Bosman AT HIS BEST

Bosman
AT HIS BEST

A CHOICE OF STORIES AND SKETCHES

BY *Herman Charles Bosman*

CULLED BY *Lionel Abrahams*

Human & Rousseau

CAPE TOWN AND PRETORIA

First published in 1965 by
Human & Rousseau Publishers (Pty.) Ltd.
3-9 Rose Street, Cape Town; 239 Pretorius Street, Pretoria
All Rights reserved

First Printing 1965
Second Printing 1967
Third Printing 1969
Fourth Printing 1970
Fifth Printing 1971
Sixth Printing 1972
Seventh Printing 1973
Eighth Printing 1974
Ninth Printing 1977

ISBN 0 7981 0249 7

Printed by National Book Printers, Goodwood

Contents

FROM *Mafeking Road* (1947)

In the Withaak's Shade

Leopards? – Oom Schalk Lourens said – Oh, yes, there are two varieties on this side of the Limpopo. The chief difference between them is that the one kind of leopard has got a few more spots on it than the other kind. But when you meet a leopard in the veld, unexpectedly, you seldom trouble to count his spots to find out what kind he belongs to. That is unnecessary. Because, whatever kind of leopard it is that you come across in this way, you only do one kind of running. And that is the fastest kind.

I remember the occasion that I came across a leopard unexpectedly, and to this day I couldn't tell you how many spots he had, even though I had all the time I needed for studying him. It happened about mid-day, when I was out on the far end of my farm, behind a koppie, looking for some strayed cattle. I thought the cattle might be there because it is shady under those withaak trees, and there is soft grass that is very pleasant to sit on. After I had looked for the cattle for about an hour in this manner, sitting up against a tree-trunk, it occurred to me that I could look for them just as well, or perhaps even better, if I lay down flat. For even a child knows that cattle aren't so small that you have got to get on to stilts and things to see them properly.

So I lay on my back, with my hat tilted over my face, and my legs crossed, and when I closed my eyes slightly the tip of my boot, sticking up into the air, looked just like the peak of Abjaterskop.

Overhead a lonely aasvoël wheeled, circling slowly round and round without flapping his wings, and I knew that not even a calf could pass in any part of the sky between the tip of my toe and that aasvoël without my observing it immediately. What was more, I could go on lying there under the withaak and looking for the cattle like that all day, if necessary. As you know, I am not the sort of farmer to loaf about the house when there is a man's work to be done.

The more I screwed up my eyes and gazed at the toe of my boot, the more it looked like Abjaterskop. By and by it seemed that it actually was Abjaterskop, and I could see the stones on top of it, and the bush trying to grow up its sides, and in my ears there was a far-off humming sound, like bees in an orchard on a still day. As I have said, it was very pleasant.

Then a strange thing happened. It was as though a huge cloud, shaped like an animal's head and with spots on it, had settled on top of Abjaterskop. It seemed so funny that I wanted to laugh. But I didn't. Instead, I opened my eyes a little more and felt glad to think that I was only dreaming. Because otherwise I would have to believe that the spotted cloud on Abjaterskop was actually a leopard, and that he was gazing at my boot. Again I wanted to laugh. But then, suddenly, I knew.

And I didn't feel so glad. For it was a leopard, all right – a large-sized, hungry-looking leopard, and he was sniffing suspiciously at my feet. I was uncomfortable. I knew that nothing I could do would ever convince that leopard that my toe was Abjaterskop. He was not that sort of leopard: I knew that without even counting the number of his spots. Instead, having finished with my feet, he started sniffing higher up. It was the most terrifying moment of my life. I wanted to get up and run for it. But I couldn't. My legs wouldn't work.

Every big-game hunter I have come across has told me the same story about how, at one time or another, he has owed his escape from lions and other wild animals to his cunning in lying down and pretending to be dead, so that the beast of prey loses interest in him and walks off. Now, as I lay there on the grass, with the leopard trying to make up his mind about me, I understood why, in such a situation, the hunter doesn't move. It's simply that he can't move. That's all. It's not his cunning that keeps him down. It's his legs.

In the meantime, the leopard had got up as far as my knees. He was studying my trousers very carefully, and I started getting embarrassed. My trousers were old and rather unfashionable. Also, at the knee, there was a torn place, from where I had climbed through a barbed-wire fence, into the thick bush, the time I saw the Government tax-collector coming over the bult before he saw me. The leopard stared at that rent in my trousers for quite a while, and my embarrassment grew. I felt I wanted to explain about the Government tax-collector and the barbed wire. I didn't want the leopard to get the impression that Schalk Lourens was the sort of man who didn't care about his personal appearance.

When the leopard got as far as my shirt, however, I felt better. It was a good blue flannel shirt that I had bought only a few weeks ago from the Indian store at Ramoutsa, and I didn't care how many strange leopards saw it. Nevertheless, I made up my mind that next time I want to lie on the grass under the withaak, looking for strayed cattle, I would first polish up my veldskoens with sheep's fat, and I would put on my black hat that I only wear to Nagmaal. I could not permit the wild animals of the neighbourhood to sneer at me.

But when the leopard reached my face I got frightened again. I knew he couldn't take exception to my shirt. But I wasn't so sure about my face. Those were terrible moments. I lay very still, afraid to open my eyes and afraid to breathe. Sniff-sniff, the huge creature went, and his breath swept over my face in hot gasps. You hear of many frightening experiences that a man has in a life-time. I have also been in quite a few perilous situations. But if you want something to make you suddenly old and to turn your hair white in a few moments, there is nothing to beat a leopard – especially when he is standing over you, with his jaws at your throat, trying to find a good place to bite.

The leopard gave a deep growl, stepped right over my body, knocked off my hat, and growled again. I opened my eyes and saw the animal moving away clumsily. But my relief didn't last long. The leopard didn't move far. Instead, he turned over and lay down next to me.

Yes, there on the grass, in the shade of the withaak, the leopard and I lay down together. The leopard lay half-curled up, on his side, with his forelegs crossed, like a dog, and whenever I tried to move away he grunted. I am sure that in the whole history of the Groot Marico there have never been two stranger companions engaged in the thankless task of looking for strayed cattle.

Next day, in Fanie Snyman's voorkamer, which was used as a post-office, I told my story to the farmers of the neighbourhood, while they were drinking coffee and waiting for the motor-lorry from Zeerust.

"And how did you get away from that leopard in the end?" Koos van Tonder asked, trying to be funny, "I suppose you crawled through the grass and frightened the leopard off by pretending to be a python."

"No, I just got up and walked home," I said. "I remembered that the cattle I was looking for might have gone the other way and strayed into your kraal. I thought they would be safer with the leopard."

"Did the leopard tell you what he thought of General Pienaar's last speech in the Volksraad?" Frans Welman asked, and they all laughed.

I told my story over several times before the lorry came with our letters, and although the dozen odd men present didn't say much while I was talking, I could see that they listened to me in the same way that they listened when Krisjan Lemmer talked. And everybody knew that Krisjan Lemmer was the biggest liar in the Bushveld.

To make matters worse, Krisjan Lemmer was there, too, and when I got to the part of my story where the leopard lay down beside me, Krisjan Lemmer winked at me. You know that kind of wink. It was to let me know that there was now a new understanding between us, and that we could speak in future as one Marico liar to another.

I didn't like that.

"Kêrels," I said in the end, "I know just what you are thinking. You don't believe me, and you don't want to say so."

"But we do believe you," Krisjan Lemmer interrupted me, "very wonderful things happen in the Bushveld. I once had a twenty-foot mamba that I named Hans. This snake was so attached to me that I couldn't go anywhere without him. He would even follow me to church on Sunday, and because he didn't care much for some of the sermons, he would wait for me outside under a tree. Not that Hans was irreligious. But he had a sensitive nature, and the strong line that the predikant took against the serpent in the Garden of Eden always made Hans feel awkward. Yet he didn't go and look for a withaak to lie under, like your leopard. He wasn't stand-offish in that way. An ordinary thorn-tree's shade was good enough for Hans. He knew he was only a mamba, and didn't try to give himself airs."

I didn't take any notice of Krisjan Lemmer's stupid lies, but the upshot of this whole affair was that I also began to have doubts about the existence of that leopard. I recalled queer stories I had heard of human beings that could turn themselves into animals, and although I am not a superstitious man I could not shake off the feeling that it was a spook thing that had happened. But when, a few days later, a huge leopard had been seen from the roadside near the poort, and then again by Mtosas on the way to Nietverdiend, and again in the turf-lands near the Malopo, matters took a different turn.

At first people jested about this leopard. They said it wasn't a real leopard, but a spotted animal that had walked away out of Schalk Lourens' dream. They also said that the leopard had come to the Dwarsberge to have a look at Krisjan Lemmer's twenty-foot mamba. But afterwards, when they had found his spoor at several water-holes, they had no more doubt about the leopard.

It was dangerous to walk about in the veld, they said. Exciting times followed. There was a great deal of shooting at the leopard and a great deal of running away from him. The amount of Martini and Mauser fire I heard in the krantzes reminded me of nothing so much as the First Boer War. And the amount of running away reminded me of nothing so much as the Second Boer War.

But always the leopard escaped unharmed. Somehow, I felt sorry for him. The way he had first sniffed at me and then lain down beside me that day under the withaak was a strange thing that I couldn't understand. I thought of the Bible, where it is written that the lion shall lie down with the lamb.

But I also wondered if I hadn't dreamt it all. The manner in which those things had befallen me was also unearthly. The leopard began to take up a lot of my thoughts. And there was no man to whom I could talk about it who would be able to help me in any way. Even now, as I am telling you this story, I am expecting you to wink at me, like Krisjan Lemmer did.

Still, I can only tell you the things that happened as I saw them, and what the rest was about only Africa knows.

It was some time before I again walked along the path that leads through the bush to where the withaaks are. But I didn't lie down on the grass again. Because when I reached the place, I found that the leopard had got there before me. He was lying on the same spot, half-curled up in the withaak's shade, and his fore-paws were folded as a dog's are, sometimes. But he lay very still. And even from the distance where I stood I could see the red splash on his breast where a Mauser bullet had gone.

Ox-Wagons on Trek

When I see the rain beating white on the thorn-trees, as it does now (Oom Schalk Lourens said) I remember another time when it rained. And there was a girl in an ox-wagon who dreamed. And in answer to her dreaming a lover came, galloping to her side from out of the veld. But he tarried only a short while, this lover who had come to her from the mist of the rain and the warmth of her dreams.

And yet when he had gone there was a slow look in her eyes that must have puzzled her lover very much for it was a look of satisfaction, almost.

There had been rain all the way up from Sephton's Nek, that time. And the five ox-wagons on the road to the north rolled heavily through the mud. We had been to Zeerust for the Nagmaal church service, which we attended once a year.

You know what it is with these Nagmaals.

The Lord spreads these festivities over so many days that you have not only got time to go to church, but you also get a chance of going to the bioscope. Sometimes you even get a chance of going to the bar. But then you must go in the back way, through the dark passage next to the draper's shop.

Because Zeerust is a small place, and if you are seen going into the bar during Nagmaal, people are liable to talk. I can still remember how surprised I was one morning when I went into that dark passage next to the draper's shop and found the predikant there, wiping his mouth. The predikant looked at me and shook his head solemnly, and I felt very guilty.

So I went to the bioscope instead.

The house was very crowded. I couldn't follow much of the picture at the beginning, but afterwards a little boy who sat next to me and understood English explained to me what it was all about.

There was a young man who had the job of what he called taking people for a ride. Afterwards he got into trouble with the police. But he was a good-looking young man, and his sweetheart was very sorry for him when they took him into a small room and fastened him down on to a sort of chair.

I can't tell what they did that for. All I know is that I have been a Boer War prisoner at St. Helena, and they never gave me a chair to sit on. Only a long wooden bench that I had to scrub once a week.

Anyway I don't know what happened to the young man after that, because he was still sitting in that chair when the band started playing an English hymn about King George, and everybody stood up.

And a few days later five ox-wagons, full of people who had been to the Zeerust Nagmaal, were trekking along the road that led back to the Groot Marico. Inside the wagon-tents sat the women and children, listening to the rain pelting against the canvas. By the side of the oxen the drivers walked, cracking their long whips while the rain beat in their faces.

Overhead everything was black, except for the frequent flashes of lightning that tore across the sky.

After I had walked in this manner for some time, I began to get lonely. So I handed my whip to the kafir voorloper and went on ahead to Adriaan Brand's wagon. For some distance I walked in silence beside Adriaan, who had his trousers rolled up to his knees, and had much trouble to brandish his whip and at the same time keep the rain out of his pipe.

"It's Minnie," Adriaan Brand said suddenly, referring to his nineteen-year-old daughter. "There is one place in Zeerust that Minnie should not go to. And every Nagmaal, to my sorrow, I find she has been there. And it all goes to her head."

"Oh, yes," I answered. "It always does."

All the same, I was somewhat startled at Adriaan's remarks. Minnie didn't strike me as the sort of girl who would go and spend her father's money drinking peach-brandy in the bar. I started wondering if she had seen me in that draper's passage. Then Adriaan went on talking and I felt more at ease.

"The place where they show those moving pictures," he explained. "Every time Minnie goes there, she comes back with ideas that are useless for a farmer's daughter. But this last time has made her quite impossible. For one thing, she says she won't marry Frans du Toit any more. She says Frans is too honest."

"Well, that needn't be a difficulty, Adriaan," I said. "You can teach Frans du Toit a few of the things you have done. That will make him dishonest enough. Like the way you put your brand on those oxen that strayed into your kraal. Or the way you altered the figures on the compensation forms after the rinderpest. Or the way – "

Adriaan looked at me with some disfavour.

"It isn't that," he interrupted me, while I was still trying to call to mind a lot of other things that he was able to teach Frans du Toit, "Minnie wants a mysterious sort of man. She wants a man who is dishonest, but who has got foreign manners and a good heart. She saw a man like that at the picture place she went to, and since then . . ."

We both looked round together.

Through the mist of the white rain a horseman came galloping up towards our wagons. He rode fast. Adriaan Brand and I stood and watched him.

By this time our wagons were some distance behind the others.

The horseman came thundering along at full gallop until he was abreast of us. Then he pulled up sharply, jerking the horse on to his hind legs.

The stranger told us that his name was Koos Fichardt and that he was on his way to the Bechuanaland Protectorate. Adriaan Brand and I introduced ourselves, and shortly afterwards Fichardt accepted our invitation to spend the night with us.

We outspanned a mile or so farther on, drawing the five wagons up close together and getting what shelter we could by spreading buck-sails.

Next morning there was no more rain. By that time Koos Fichardt had seen Adriaan Brand's daughter Minnie. So he decided to stay with us longer.

We trekked on again, and from where I walked beside my oxen I could see Koos Fichardt and Minnie. They sat at the back of

Adriaan Brand's wagon, hatless, with their legs hanging down and the morning breeze blowing through their hair, and it was evident that Minnie was fascinated by the stranger. Also, he seemed to be very much interested in her.

You do get like that, when there is suddenly a bright morning after long rains, and a low wind stirs the wet grass, and you feel, for a little while, that you know the same thing that the veld knows, and in your heart are whisperings.

Most of the time they sat holding hands, Fichardt talking a great deal and Minnie nodding her pretty head at intervals and encouraging him to continue. And they were all lies he told her, I suppose, as only a young man in love really can tell lies.

I remembered what Adriaan told me about the ideas Minnie had got after she had been to the bioscope. And when I looked carefully at Fichardt I perceived that in many respects he was like that man I saw in the picture who was being fastened on to a chair.

Fichardt was tall and dark and well-dressed. He walked with a swagger. He had easy and engaging manners, and we all liked him.

But I noticed one or two peculiar things about Koos Fichardt. For instance, shortly after our wagons had entered a clump of tall camel-thorn trees, we heard horse-hoofs galloping towards us. It turned out that the riders were a couple of farmers living in the neighbourhood. But as soon as he heard the hoof-beats, Koos Fichardt let go of Minnie's hand and crept under a bucksail.

It would be more correct to say that he dived under – he was so quick.

I said to myself that Fichardt's action might have no meaning, of course. After all, it is quite permissible for a man to feel that he would suddenly like to take a look at what is underneath the bucksail he is sitting on. Also, if he wants to, there is no harm in his spending quite a while on this task. And it is only natural, after he has had a bucksail on top of him, that he should come out with his hair rather ruffled, and that his face should be pale.

That night, when we outspanned next to the Groen River, it was very pleasant. We all gathered round the camp-fire and roasted meat and cooked crushed mealies. We sang songs and told ghost stories. And I wondered what Frans du Toit – the honest youth whom Minnie had discarded in Zeerust – would have thought if he could see Minnie Brand and Koos Fichardt, sitting unashamedly in each other's arms, for all the world to see their love, while the light of the camp-fire cast a rich glow over the thrill that was on their faces.

And although I knew how wonderful were the passing moments for those two, yet somehow, somehow, because I had seen so much of the world, I also felt sorry for them.

The next day we did not trek.

The Groen River was in flood from the heavy rains, and Oupa van Tonder, who had lived a long time in the Cape and was well versed in the ways of rivers, and knew how to swim even, told us that it would not be safe to cross the drift for another twenty-four hours. Accordingly, we decided to remain camped out where we were until next morning.

At first Koos Fichardt was much disturbed by this news, explaining how necessary it was for him to get into the Bechuanaland Protectorate by a certain day. After a while, however, he seemed to grow more reconciled to the necessity of waiting until the river had gone down.

But I noticed that he frequently gazed out over the veld in the direction from which we had come. He gazed out rather anxiously, I thought.

Some of the men went shooting. Others remained at their wagons, doing odd jobs to the yokes or the trek chains. Koos Fichardt made himself useful in various little ways, amongst other things, helping Minnie with the cooking. They laughed and romped a good deal.

Night came, and the occupants of the five wagons again gathered round the blazing fire. In some ways, that night was even grander than the one before. The songs we sang were more rousing. The stories we told seemed to have more power in them.

There was much excitement the following morning by the time the wagons were ready to go through the drift. And the excitement did not lie only in the bustle of inspanning the oxen.

For when we crossed the river it was without Koos Fichardt, and there was a slow look in Minnie's eyes.

The wagons creaked and splashed in the water, and we saw

Koos Fichardt for the last time, sitting on his horse, with a horse-man in uniform on each side of him. And when he took off his hat in farewell he had to use both hands, because of the cuffs that held his wrists together.

But always what I will remember is that slow look in Minnie's eyes. It was a kind of satisfaction, almost, at the thought that all the things that came to the girl she saw in the picture had now come to her, too.

The Music-Maker

Of course, I know about history – Oom Schalk Lourens said – it's the stuff children learn in school. Only the other day, at Thys Lemmer's post office, Thys's little son Stoffel started reading out of his history book about a man called Vasco da Gama, who visited the Cape. At once Dirk Snyman started telling young Stoffel about the time when he himself visited the Cape, but young Stoffel didn't take much notice of him. So Dirk Snyman said that that showed you.

Anyway, Dirk Snyman said that what he wanted to tell young Stoffel was that the last time he went down to the Cape a kafir came and sat down right next to him in a tram. What was more, Dirk Snyman said, was that people seemed to think nothing of it.

Yes, it's a queer thing about wanting to get into history.

Take the case of Manie Kruger, for instance.

Manie Kruger was one of the best farmers in the Marico. He knew just how much peach-brandy to pour out for the tax-collector to make sure that he would nod dreamily at everything Manie said. And at a time of drought Manie Kruger could run to the Government for help much quicker than any man I ever knew.

Then one day Manie Kruger read an article in the *Kerkbode* about a musician who said that he knew more about music than Napoleon did. After that – having first read another article to find out who Napoleon was – Manie Kruger was a changed man. He could talk of nothing but his place in history and of his musical career.

Of course, everybody knew that no man in the Marico could be counted in the same class with Manie Kruger when it came to playing the concertina.

No Bushveld dance was complete without Manie Kruger's concertina. When he played a vastrap you couldn't keep your feet still. But after he had decided to become the sort of musician that gets into history books, it was strange the way that Manie Kruger altered. For one thing, he said he would never again play at a dance. We all felt sad about that. It was not easy to think of the Bushveld dances of the future. There would be the peach-brandy in the kitchen; in the voorkamer the feet of the dancers would go through the steps of the schottische and the polka and the waltz and the mazurka, but on the riempies bench in the corner where the musicians sat, there would be no Manie Kruger. And they would play "Die Vaal Hare en die Blou Oge" and "Vat Jou Goed en Trek, Ferreira," but it would be another's fingers that swept over the concertina keys. And when, with the dancing and the peach-brandy, the young men called out "Dagbreek toe" it would not be Manie Kruger's head that bowed down to the applause.

It was sad to think about all this.

For so long, at the Bushveld dances, Manie Kruger had been the chief musician.

And of all those who mourned this change that had come over Manie, we could see that there was no one more grieved than Letta Steyn.

And Manie said such queer things at times. Once he said that what he had to do to get into history was to die of consumption in the arms of a princess, like another musician he had read about. Only it was hard to get consumption in the Marico, because the climate was so healthy.

Although Manie stopped playing his concertina at dances, he played a great deal in another way. He started giving what he called recitals. I went to several of them. They were very impressive.

At the first recital I went to, I found that the front part of Manie's voorkamer was taken up by rows of benches and chairs that he had borrowed from those of his neighbours who didn't mind having to eat their meals on candle-boxes and upturned buckets. At the far end of the voorkamer a wide green curtain was hung on a piece of string. When I came in the place was full. I managed to squeeze in on a bench between Jan Terblanche and a young woman in a blue kappie. Jan Terblanche had been trying to hold this young woman's hand.

Manie Kruger was sitting behind the green curtain. He was already there when I came in. I knew it was Manie by his veldskoens, which were sticking out from underneath the curtain. Letta Steyn sat in front of me. Now and again, when she turned round, I saw that there was a flush on her face and a look of dark excitement in her eyes.

At last everything was ready, and Joel, the farm kafir to whom Manie had given this job, slowly drew the green curtain aside. A few of the younger men called out "Middag, ou Manie," and Jan Terblanche asked if it wasn't very close and suffocating, sitting there like that behind that piece of green curtain.

Then he started to play.

And we all knew that it was the most wonderful concertina music we had ever listened to. It was Manie Kruger at his best. He had practised a long time for that recital; his fingers flew over the keys; the notes of the concertina swept into our hearts; the music of Manie Kruger lifted us right out of that voorkamer into a strange and rich and dazzling world.

It was fine.

The applause right through was terrific. At the end of each piece the kafir closed the curtains in front of Manie, and we sat waiting for a few minutes until the curtains were drawn aside again. But after that first time there was no more laughter about this procedure. The recital lasted for about an hour and a half, and the applause at the end was even greater than at the start. And during those ninety minutes Manie left his seat only once. That was when there was some trouble with the curtain and he got up to kick the kafir.

At the end of the recital Manie did not come forward and shake hands with us, as we had expected. Instead, he slipped through behind the green curtain into the kitchen, and sent word that we could come and see him round the back. At first we thought this a bit queer, but Letta Steyn said it was all right. She explained that in other countries the great musicians and stage performers all received their admirers at the back. Jan Terblanche said that if these actors used their kitchens for entertaining their visitors in, he wondered where they did their cooking.

Nevertheless, most of us went round to the kitchen, and we had a good time congratulating Manie Kruger and shaking hands with him; and Manie spoke much of his musical future, and of the triumphs that would come to him in the great cities of the world, when he would stand before the curtain and bow to the applause.

Manie gave a number of other recitals after that. They were all equally fine. Only, as he had to practise all day, he couldn't pay much attention to his farming. The result was that his farm went to pieces and he got into debt. The court messengers came and attached half his cattle while he was busy practising for his fourth recital. And he was practising for his seventh recital when they took away his ox-wagon and mule-cart.

Eventually, when Manie Kruger's musical career reached that stage when they took away his plough and the last of his oxen, he sold up what remained of his possessions and left the Bushveld, on his way to those great cities that he had so often talked about. It was very grand, the send-off that the Marico gave him. The predikant and the Volksraad member both made speeches about how proud the Transvaal was of her great son. Then Manie replied. Instead of thanking his audience, however, he started abusing us left and right, calling us a mob of hooligans and soul-less Philistines, and saying how much he despised us.

Naturally, we were very much surprised at this outburst, as we had always been kind to Manie Kruger and had encouraged him all we could. But Letta Steyn explained that Manie didn't really mean the things he said. She said it was just that every great artist was expected to talk in that way about the place he came from.

So we knew it was all right, and the more offensive the things were that Manie said about us, the louder we shouted "Hoor, hoor vir Manie." There was a particularly enthusiastic round of applause when he said that we knew as much about art as a boom-slang. His language was hotter than anything I had ever heard — except once. And that was when de Wet said what he thought of Cronje's surrender to the English at Paardeberg. We could feel that Manie's speech was the real thing. We cheered ourselves hoarse, that day.

And so Manie Kruger went. We received one letter to say that he had reached Pretoria. But after that we heard no more from him.

Yet always, when Letta Steyn spoke of Manie, it was as a child speaks of a dream, half wistfully, and always, with the voice of a wistful child, she would tell me how one day, one day he would return. And often, when it was dusk, I would see her sitting on the stoep, gazing out across the veld into the evening, down the dusty road that led between the thorn-trees and beyond the Dwarsberg, waiting for the lover who would come to her no more.

It was a long time before I again saw Manie Kruger. And then it was in Pretoria. I had gone there to interview the Volksraad member about an election promise. It was quite by accident that I saw Manie. And he was playing the concertina – playing as well as ever, I thought. I went away quickly. But what affected me very strangely was just that one glimpse I had of the green curtain of the bar in front of which Manie Kruger played.

Mafeking Road

When people ask me – as they often do, how it is that I can tell the best stories of anybody in the Transvaal (Oom Schalk Lourens said, modestly), then I explain to them that I just learn through observing the way that the world has with men and women. When I say this they nod their heads wisely, and say that they understand, and I nod my head wisely also, and that seems to satisfy them. But the thing I say to them is a lie, of course.

For it is not the story that counts. What matters is the way you tell it. The important thing is to know just at what moment you must knock out your pipe on your veldskoen, and at what stage of the story you must start talking about the School Committee at Drogevlei. Another necessary thing is to know what part of the story to leave out.

And you can never learn these things.

Look at Floris, the last of the Van Barnevelts. There is no doubt that he had a good story, and he should have been able to get people to listen to it. And yet nobody took any notice of him or of the things he had to say. Just because he couldn't tell the story properly.

Accordingly, it made me sad whenever I listened to him talk. For I could tell just where he went wrong. He never knew the moment at which to knock the ash out of his pipe. He always mentioned his opinion of the Drogevlei School Committee in the wrong place. And, what was still worse, he didn't know what part of the story to leave out.

And it was no use my trying to teach him, because as I have said, this is the thing that you can never learn. And so, each time he had told his story, I would see him turn away from me, with a look of doom on his face, and walk slowly down the road, stoop-shouldered, the last of the Van Barnevelts.

On the wall of Floris' voorkamer is a long family tree of the Van Barnevelts. You can see it there for yourself. It goes back for over two hundred years, to the Van Barnevelts of Amsterdam. At one time it went even further back, but that was before the white ants started on the top part of it and ate away quite a lot of Van Barnevelts. Nevertheless, if you look at this list, you will notice that at the bottom under Floris' own name, there is the last entry, "Stephanus". And behind the name, "Stephanus", between two bent strokes, you will read the words: "Obiit Mafeking".

At the outbreak of the Second Boer War Floris Van Barnevelt was a widower, with one son, Stephanus, who was aged seventeen. The commando from our part of the Transvaal set off very cheerfully. We made a fine show with our horses and our wide hats, and our bandoliers, and with the sun shining on the barrels of our Mausers.

Young Stephanus van Barnevelt was the gayest of us all. But he said there was one thing he didn't like about the war, and that was that, in the end, we would have to go over the sea. He said that, after we had invaded the whole of the Cape, our commando would have to go on a ship and invade England also.

But we didn't go overseas, just then. Instead, our veld-kornet told us that the burghers from our part had been ordered to join the big commando that was lying at Mafeking. We had to go and shoot a man there called Baden-Powell.

We rode steadily on into the west. After a while we noticed that our veld-kornet frequently got off his horse and engaged in conversation with passing kafirs, leading them some distance from the roadside and speaking earnestly to them. Of course, it was right that our veld-kornet should explain to the kafirs that it was wartime, now, and that the Republic expected every kafir to stop smoking so much dagga and to think seriously about what was going on.

But we noticed that each time at the end of the conversation the kafir would point towards something, and that our veld-kornet would take much pains to follow the direction of the kafir's finger.

Of course, we understood, then, what it was all about. Our veld-kornet was a young fellow, and he was shy to let us see that he didn't know the way to Mafeking.

Somehow, after that, we did not have so much confidence in our veld-kornet.

After a few days we got to Mafeking. We stayed there a long while, until the English troops came up and relieved the place. We left then. We left quickly. The English troops had brought a lot of artillery with them. And if we had difficulty in finding the road to Mafeking, we had no difficulty in finding the road away from Mafeking. And this time our veld-kornet did not need kafirs, either, to point with their fingers where we had to go. Even though we did a lot of travelling in the night.

Long afterwards I spoke to an Englishman about this. He said it gave him a queer feeling to hear about the other side of the story of Mafeking. He said there had been very great rejoicings in England when Mafeking was relieved, and it was strange to think of the other aspect of it — of a defeated country and of broken columns blundering through the dark.

I remember many things that happened on the way back from Mafeking. There was no moon. And the stars shone down fitfully on the road that was full of guns and frightened horses and desperate men. The veld throbbed with the hoof-beats of baffled commandos. The stars looked down on scenes that told sombrely of a nation's ruin; they looked on the muzzles of the Mausers that had failed the Transvaal for the first time.

Of course, as a burgher of the Republic, I knew what my duty was. And that was to get as far away as I could from the place where, in the sunset, I had last seen English artillery. The other burghers knew their duty also. Our commandants and veld-kornets had to give very few orders. Nevertheless, although I rode very fast, there was one young man who rode still faster. He kept ahead of me all the time. He rode, as a burgher should ride when there may be stray bullets flying, with his head well down and with his arms almost round the horse's neck.

He was Stephanus, the young son of Floris van Barnevelt.

There was much grumbling and dissatisfaction, some time afterwards, when our leaders started making an effort to get the commandos in order again. In the end they managed to get us to halt. But most of us felt that this was a foolish thing to do. Especially as there was still a lot of firing going on, all over the place, in haphazard fashion, and we couldn't tell how far the English had followed us in the dark. Furthermore, the commandos had scattered in so many different directions that it seemed hopeless to try and get them together again until after the war. Stephanus and I dismounted and stood by our horses. Soon there was a large body of men around us. Their figures looked strange and shadowy in the starlight. Some of them stood by their horses. Others sat on the grass by the roadside. "Vas staan, Burghers, vas staan," came the commands of our officers. And all the time we could still hear what sounded a lot like lyddite. It seemed foolish to be waiting there.

"The next they'll want," Stephanus van Barnevelt said, "is for us to go back to Mafeking. Perhaps our commandant has left his tobacco pouch behind, there."

Some of us laughed at this remark, but Floris, who had not dismounted, said that Stephanus ought to be ashamed of himself for talking like that. From what we could see of Floris in the gloom, he looked quite impressive, sitting very straight in the saddle, with the stars shining on his beard and rifle.

"If the veld-kornet told me to go back to Mafeking," Floris said, "I would go back."

"That's how a burgher should talk," the veld-kornet said, feeling flattered. For he had had little authority since the time we found out what he was talking to the kafirs for.

"I wouldn't go back to Mafeking for anybody," Stephanus replied, "unless, maybe, it's to hand myself over to the English."

"We can shoot you for doing that," the veld-kornet said. "It's contrary to military law."

"I wish I knew something about military law," Stephanus answered. "Then I would draw up a peace treaty between Stephanus van Barnevelt and England."

Some of the men laughed again. But Floris shook his head sadly. He said the Van Barnevelts had fought bravely against Spain in a war that lasted eighty years.

Suddenly, out of the darkness there came a sharp rattle of musketry, and our men started getting uneasy again. But the sound of the firing decided Stephanus. He jumped on his horse quickly.

"I am turning back," he said, "I am going to hands-up to the English."

"No, don't go," the veld-kornet called to him lamely, "or at least, wait until the morning. They may shoot you in the dark by mistake." As I have said the veld-kornet had very little authority.

Two days passed before we again saw Floris van Barnevelt. He was in a very worn and troubled state, and he said that it had been very hard for him to find his way back to us.

"You should have asked the kafirs," one of our number said with a laugh. "All the kafirs know our veld-kornet."

But Floris did not speak about what happened that night, when we saw him riding out under the star-light, following after his son and shouting to him to be a man and to fight for his country. Also, Floris did not mention Stephanus again, his son who was not worthy to be a Van Barnevelt.

After that we got separated. Our veld-kornet was the first to be taken prisoner. And I often felt that he must feel very lonely on St. Helena. Because there were no kafirs from whom he could ask the way out of the barbed-wire camp.

Then, at last our leaders came together at Vereeniging, and peace was made. And we returned to our farms, relieved that the war was over, but with heavy hearts at the thought that it had all been for nothing and that over the Transvaal the Vierkleur would not wave again.

And Floris van Barnevelt put back in its place, on the wall of the voorkamer, the copy of his family tree that had been carried with him in his knapsack throughout the war. Then a new school-master came to this part of the Marico, and after a long talk with Floris, the schoolmaster wrote, behind Stephanus' name, between two curved lines, the two words that you can still read there: "Obiit Mafeking".

Consequently, if you ask any person hereabouts what "obiit" means he is able to tell you, right away, that it is a foreign word, and that it means to ride up to the English, holding your Mauser in the air, with a white flag tied to it, near the muzzle.

But it was long afterwards that Floris van Barnevelt started telling his story.

And then they took no notice of him. And they wouldn't allow him to be nominated for the Drogevlei School Committee on the grounds that a man must be wrong in the head to talk in such an irresponsible fashion.

But I knew that Floris had a good story, and that its only fault was that he told it badly. He mentioned the Drogevlei School Committee too soon. And he knocked the ash out of his pipe in the wrong place. And he always insisted on telling that part of the story that he should have left out.

The Prophet

No, I never came across the Prophet van Rensburg, the man who told General Kemp that it was the right time to rebel against the English. As you know, General Kemp followed his advice and they say that General Kemp still believed in Van Rensburg's prophecies, even after the two of them were locked up in the Pretoria Gaol.

But I knew another prophet. His name was Erasmus. Stephanus Erasmus. Van Rensburg could only foretell that so and so was going to happen, and then he was wrong sometimes. But with Stephanus Erasmus it was different. Erasmus used to make things come true just by prophesying them.

You can see what that means. And yet, in the end I wondered about Stephanus Erasmus.

There are lots of people like Van Rensburg who can just foretell the future, but when a man comes along who can actually make the future, then you feel that you can't make jokes about him. All the farmers in Drogedal talked about Stephanus Erasmus with respect. Even when he wasn't present to hear what was being said about him. Because there would always be somebody to go along and tell him if you happen to make some slighting remark about him.

I know, because once in Piet Fourie's house I said that if I was a great Prophet like Stephanus Erasmus I would try and prophesy myself a new pair of veldskoens, seeing that his were all broken on top and you could see two corns and part of an ingrowing toenail. After that things went all wrong on my farm for six months. So I knew that Piet Fourie had told the prophet what I had said. Amongst other things six of my best trek-oxen died of the miltsiekte.

After that, whenever I wanted to think anything unflattering about Stephanus Erasmus I went right out into the veld and did it all there. You can imagine that round that time I went into the veld alone very often. It wasn't easy to forget about the six trek-oxen.

More than once I hoped that Stephanus Erasmus would also take it into his head to tell General Kemp that it was the right time to go into rebellion. But Erasmus was too wise for that. I remember once when we were all together just before a meeting of the Dwarsberg School Committee I asked Stephanus about this.

"What do you think of this new wheel-tax, Oom Stephanus?" I said. "Don't you think the people should go along with their rifles and hoist the vierkleur over the magistrate's courts at Zeerust?"

Erasmus looked at me and I lowered my eyes. I felt sorry in a way that I had spoken. His eyes seemed to look right through me. I felt that to him I looked like a springbok that had been shot and cut open, and you can see his heart and his ribs and his liver and his stomach and all the rest of his inside. It is not very pleasant to be sitting talking to a man who regards you as nothing more than a cut-open springbok.

But Stephanus Erasmus went on looking at me. I became frightened. If he had said to me then, "You know you are just a cut-open springbok," I would have said, "Yes, Oom Stephanus, I know." I could see then that he had a great power. He was just an ordinary sort of farmer on the outside, with a black beard and dark eyes and a pair of old shoes that were broken on top. But inside he was terrible. I began to be afraid for my remaining trek-oxen.

Then he spoke, slowly and with wisdom.

"There are also magistrates' courts at Mafeking and Zwartruggens and Rysmierbult," he said. "In fact there is a magistrate's court in every town I have been in along the railway line. And all these magistrate's courts collect wheel-tax," Oom Stephanus said.

I could see then that he not only had great power inside him, but that he was also very cunning. He never went in for any wild guessing, like saying to a stranger, "You are a married man with five children and in your inside jacket-pocket is a letter from the Kerkraad asking you to become an ouderling." I have seen some so-called fortune-tellers say that to a man they had never seen in their lives before in the hope that they might be right.

You know, it is a wonderful thing this, about being a Prophet. I have thought much about it, and what I know about it I can't explain. But I know it has got something to do with death. This is one of the things I have learnt in the Marico, and I don't think you could learn it anywhere else. It is only when you have had a great deal of time in which to do nothing but think and look at the veld and at the sky where there have been no rain-clouds for many months, that you grow to an understanding of these things.

Then you know that being a prophet and having power is very simple. But it is also something very terrible. And you know then that there are men and women who are unearthly, and it is this that makes them greater than kings. For a king can lose his power when people take it away from him, but a prophet can never lose his power — if he is a real prophet.

It was the school-children who first began talking about this. I have noticed how often things like this start with the stories of kafirs and children.

Anyway, a very old kafir had come to live at the outspan on the road to Ramoutsa. Nobody knew where he had come from, except that when questioned he would lift up his arm very slowly and point towards the west. There is nothing in the west. There is only the Kalahari Desert. And from his looks you could easily believe that this old kafir had lived in the desert all his life. There was something about his withered body that reminded you of the Great Drought.

We found out that this kafir's name was Mosiko. He had made himself a rough shelter of thorn-bushes and old mealie bags. And there he lived alone.

The kafirs round about brought him mealies and beer, and from what they told us it appeared that he was not very grateful for these gifts, and when the beer was weak he swore vilely at the persons who brought it.

As I have said, it was the kafirs who first took notice of him. They said he was a great witch-doctor. But later on white people also started taking him presents. And they asked him questions about what was going to happen. Sometimes Mosiko told them what they wanted to know. At other times he was impudent and told them to go and ask Baas Stephanus Erasmus.

You can imagine what a stir this created.

"Yes," Frans Steyn said to us one afternoon. "And when I asked this kafir whether my daughter Anna should get married to Gert right away or whether she should go to High School to learn English, Mosiko said that I had to ask Baas Stephanus. 'Ask him,' he said, 'that one is too easy for me.'"

Then the people said that this Mosiko was an impertinent kafir and that the only thing Stephanus could do was not to take any notice of him.

I watched closely to see what Erasmus was going to do about it. I could see that the kafir's impudence was making him mad. And when people said to him, "Do not take any notice of Mosiko, Oom Stephanus, he is a lazy old kafir," anyone could see that this annoyed him more than anything else. He suspected that they said this out of politeness. And there is nothing that angers you more than when those who used to fear you start being polite to you.

The upshot of the business was that Stephanus Erasmus went to the outspan where Mosiko lived. He said he was going to boot him back into the Kalahari, where he came from. Now, it was a mistake for Stephanus to have gone out to see Mosiko. For Mosiko looked really important to have the prophet coming to visit him. The right thing always is for the servant to visit the master.

All of us went along with Stephanus.

On the way down he said, "I'll kick him all the way out of Zeerust. It is bad enough when kafirs wear collars and ties in Johannesburg and walk on the pavements reading newspapers. But we can't allow this sort of thing in the Marico."

But I could see that for some reason Stephanus was growing angry and he tried to pretend that we were determined to have Mosiko shown up. And this was not the truth. It was only Erasmus's quarrel. It was not our affair at all.

We got to the outspan.

Mosiko had hardly any clothes on. He sat up against a bush with his back bent and his head forward near his knees. He had many wrinkles. Hundreds of them. He looked to be the oldest man in the world. And yet there was a kind of strength about the curve of his back and I knew the meaning of it. It seemed to me that with his back curved in that way, and the sun shining on him and his head bent forward, Mosiko could be much greater and do more things just by sitting down than other men could do by working hard and using cunning. I felt that Mosiko could sit down and do nothing and yet be more powerful than the Commandant-General.

He seemed to have nothing but what the sun and the sand and the grass had given him, and yet that was more than what all the men in the world could give him.

I was glad that I was there that day, at the meeting of the wizards.

Stephanus Erasmus knew who Mosiko was, of course. But I wasn't sure if Mosiko knew Stephanus. So I introduced them. On another day people would have laughed at the way I did it. But at that moment it didn't seem so funny, somehow.

"Mosiko," I said, "this is Baas Prophet Stephanus Erasmus."

"And, Oom Stephanus," I said, "this is Witch-Doctor Mosiko."

Mosiko raised his eyes slightly and glanced at Erasmus. Erasmus looked straight back at Mosiko and tried to stare him out of countenance. I knew the power with which Stephanus Erasmus could look at you. So I wondered what was going to happen. But Mosiko looked down again, and kept his eyes down on the sand.

Now, I remembered how I felt that day when Stephanus Erasmus had looked at me and I was ready to believe that I was a cut-open springbok. So I was not surprised at Mosiko's turning away his eyes. But in the same moment I realised that Mosiko looked down in the way that seemed to mean that he didn't think that Stephanus was a man of enough importance for him to want to stare out of countenance. It was as though he thought there were other things for him to do but look at Stephanus.

Then Mosiko spoke.

"Tell me what you want to know, Baas Stephanus," he said, "and I'll prophesy for you."

I saw the grass and the veld and the stones. I saw a long splash of sunlight on Mosiko's naked back. But for a little while I neither saw nor heard anything else. For it was a deadly thing that the kafir had said to the white man. And I knew that the others also felt it was a deadly thing. We stood there, waiting. I was not sure whether to be glad or sorry that I had come. The time seemed so very long in passing.

"Kafir," Stephanus said at last, "you have no right to be here on a white man's outspan. We have come to throw you off it. I am going to kick you, kafir. Right now I am going to kick you. You'll see what a white man's boot is like."

Mosiko did not move. It did not seem as though he had heard anything Stephanus had said to him. He appeared to be thinking of something else – something very old and very far away.

Then Stephanus took a step forward. He paused for a moment. We all looked down.

Frans Steyn was the first to laugh. It was strange and unnatural at first to hear Frans Steyn's laughter. Everything up till then had been so tense and even frightening. But immediately afterwards we all burst out laughing together. We laughed loudly and uproariously. You could have heard us right at the other side of the bult.

I have told you about Stephanus Erasmus's veldskoens, and that they were broken on top. Well, now in walking to the outspan, the last riem had burst loose, and Stephanus Erasmus stood there with his right foot raised from the ground and a broken shoe dangling from his instep.

Stephanus never kicked Mosiko. When we had finished laughing we got him to come back home. Stephanus walked slowly, carrying the broken shoe in his hand and picking the soft places to walk on, where the burnt grass wouldn't stick into his bare foot.

Stephanus Erasmus had lost his power.

But I knew that even if his shoe hadn't broken, Stephanus would never have kicked Mosiko. I could see by that look in his eyes that, when he took the step forward and Mosiko didn't move, Stephanus had been beaten for always.

The Rooinek

Rooineks, said Oom Schalk Lourens, are queer. For instance, there was that day when my nephew Hannes and I had dealings with a couple of Englishmen near Dewetsdorp. It was shortly after Sanna's Post, and Hannes and I were lying behind a rock watching the road. Hannes spent odd moments like that in what he called a useful way. He would file the points of his Mauser cartridges on a piece of flat stone until the lead showed through the steel, in that way making them into dum-dum bullets.

I often spoke to my nephew Hannes about that.

"Hannes," I used to say. "That is a sin. The Lord is looking at you."

"That's all right," Hannes replied. "The Lord knows that this is the Boer War, and in war-time he will always forgive a little foolishness like this, especially as the English are so many."

Anyway, as we lay behind that rock we saw, far down the road, two horsemen come galloping up. We remained perfectly still and let them approach to within four hundred paces. They were English officers. They were mounted on first-rate horses and their uniforms looked very fine and smart. They were the most stylish-looking men I had seen for some time, and I felt quite ashamed of my own ragged trousers and veldskoens. I was glad that I was behind a rock and they couldn't see me. Especially as my jacket was also torn all the way down the back, as a result of my having had three days before, to get through a barbed-wire fence rather quickly. I just got through in time, too. The veld-kornet, who was a fat man and couldn't run so fast, was about twenty yards behind me. And he remained on the wire with a bullet through him. All through the Boer War I was pleased that I was thin and never troubled with corns.

Hannes and I fired just about the same time. One of the officers fell off his horse. He struck the road with his shoulders and rolled over twice, kicking up the red dust as he turned. Then the other soldier did a queer thing. He drew up his horse and got off. He gave just one look in our direction. Then he led his horse up to where the other man was twisting and struggling on the ground. It took him a little while to lift him on to his horse, for it is no easy matter to pick up a man like that when he is helpless. And he did all this slowly and calmly, as though he was not concerned about the fact that the men who had just shot his friend were lying only a few hundred yards away. He managed in some way to support the wounded man across the saddle, and walked on beside the horse. After going a few yards he stopped and seemed to remember something. He turned round and waved at the spot where he imagined we were hiding, as though inviting us to shoot. During all that time I had simply lain watching him, astonished at his coolness.

But when he waved his hand I thrust another cartridge into the breech of my Martini and aimed. I aimed very carefully and was just on the point of pulling the trigger when Hannes put his hand on the barrel and pushed up my rifle.

"Don't shoot, Oom Schalk," he said. "That's a brave man."

I looked at Hannes in surprise. His face was very white. I said nothing, and allowed my rifle to sink down on to the grass, but I couldn't understand what had come over my nephew. It seemed that not only was that Englishman queer, but that Hannes was also queer. That's all nonsense not killing a man just because he's brave. If he's a brave man and he's fighting on the wrong side, that's all the more reason to shoot him.

I was with my nephew Hannes for another few months after that. Then one day, in a skirmish near the Vaal River, Hannes with a few dozen other burghers was cut off from the commando and had to surrender. That was the last I ever saw of him. I heard later on that, after taking him prisoner, the English searched Hannes and found dum-dum bullets in his possession. They shot him for that. I was very much grieved when I heard of Hannes' death. He had always been full of life and high spirits. Perhaps Hannes was right in saying that the Lord didn't mind about a little foolishness like dum-dum bullets. But the mistake he made was in forgetting that the English did mind.

I was in the veld until they made peace. Then we laid down our rifles and went home. What I knew my farm by was the hole under the koppie where I quarried slate-stones for the threshing-floor. That was about all that remained as I left it. Everything else was gone. My home was burnt down. My lands were laid waste. My cattle and sheep were slaughtered. Even the stones I had piled for the kraals were pulled down. My wife came out of the concentration camp and we went together to look at our old farm. My wife had gone into the concentration camp with our two children, but she came out alone. And when I saw her again and noticed the way she had changed, I knew that I, who had been through all the fighting, had not seen the Boer War.

Neither Sannie nor I had the heart to go on farming again on that same place. It would be different without the children playing about the house and getting into mischief. We got paid out some money by the new Government for part of our losses. So I bought a wagon and oxen and we left the Free State, which was not even the Free State any longer. It was now called the Orange River Colony.

We trekked right through the Transvaal into the northern part of the Marico Bushveld. Years ago, as a boy, I had trekked through that same country with my parents. Now that I went there again I felt that it was still a good country. It was on the far side of the Dwarsberge, near Derdepoort, that we got a Government farm. Afterwards other farmers trekked in there as well. One or two of them had also come from the Free State, and I knew them. There were also a few Cape rebels whom I had seen on commando. All of us had lost relatives in the war. Some had died in the concentration camps or on the battlefield. Others had been shot for going into rebellion. So, taken all in all, we who trekked into that part of the Marico that lay nearest the Bechuanaland border were bitter against the English.

Then it was that the rooinek came.

It was in the first year of our having settled around Derdepoort. We heard that an Englishman had bought a farm next to Gerhardus Grobbelaar. This was when we were sitting in the voorkamer of Willem Odendaal's house, which was used as a post office. Once a week the post-cart came up with letters from Zeerust, and we came together at Willem Odendaal's house and talked and smoked and drank coffee. Very few of us ever got letters, and then it was mostly demands to pay for the boreholes that had been drilled on our farms or for cement and fencing materials. But every week regularly we went for the post. Sometimes the post-cart didn't come, because the Groen River was in flood, and we would most of us have gone home without noticing it, if somebody didn't speak about it.

When Koos Steyn heard that an Englishman was coming to live amongst us he got up from the riempies bank.

"No, kêrels," he said, "always when the Englishman comes, it means that a little later the Boer has got to shift. I'll pack up my wagon and make coffee, and just trek first thing to-morrow morning."

Most of us laughed then. Koos Steyn often said funny things like that. But some didn't laugh. Somehow, there seemed to be too much truth in Koos Steyn's words.

We discussed the matter and decided that if we Boers in the Marico could help it the rooinek would not stay amongst us too long. About half an hour later one of Willem Odendaal's children came in and said that there was a strange wagon coming along the big road. We went to the door and looked out. As the wagon came nearer we saw that it was piled up with all kinds of furniture and also sheets of iron and farming implements. There was so much stuff on the wagon that the tent had to be taken off to get everything on.

The wagon rolled along and came to a stop in front of the house. With the wagon there were one white man and two kafirs. The white man shouted something to the kafirs and threw down the whip. Then he walked up to where we were standing. He was dressed just as we were, in shirt and trousers and veldskoens, and he had dust all over him. But when he stepped over a thornbush we saw that he had got socks on. Therefore we knew that he was an Englishman.

Koos Steyn was standing in front of the door.

The Englishman went up to him and held out his hand. "Good afternoon," he said in Afrikaans. "My name is Webber."

Koos shook hands with him.

"My name is Prince Lord Alfred Milner," Koos Steyn said.

That was when Lord Milner was Governor of the Transvaal, and we all laughed. The rooinek also laughed.

41

"Well, Lord Prince," he said, "I can speak your language a little, and I hope that later on I'll be able to speak it better. I'm coming to live here, and I hope that we'll all be friends."

He then came round to all of us, but the others turned away and refused to shake hands with him. He came up to me last of all; I felt sorry for him, and although his nation had dealt unjustly with my nation and I had lost both my children in the concentration camp, still it was not so much the fault of this Englishman. It was the fault of the English Government, who wanted our gold mines. And it was also the fault of Queen Victoria, who didn't like Oom Paul Kruger, because they say that when he went over to London Oom Paul spoke to her only once for a few minutes. Oom Paul Kruger said that he was a married man and he was afraid of widows.

When the Englishman Webber went back to his wagon Koos Steyn and I walked with him. He told us that he had bought the farm next to Gerhardus Grobbelaar and that he didn't know much about sheep and cattle and mealies, but he had bought a few books on farming, and he was going to learn all he could out of them. When he said that I looked away towards the poort. I didn't want him to see that I was laughing. But with Koos Steyn it was otherwise.

"Man," he said, "let me see those books."

Webber opened the box at the bottom of the wagon and took out about six big books with green covers.

"These are very good books," Koos Steyn said. "Yes they are very good for the white ants. The white ants will eat them all in two nights."

As I have told you, Koos Steyn was a funny fellow, and no man could help laughing at the things he said.

Those were bad times. There was drought, and we could not sow mealies. The dams dried up, and there was only last year's grass on the veld. We had to pump water out of the borehole for weeks at a time. Then the rains came and for a while things were better.

Now and again I saw Webber. From what I heard about him it seemed that he was working hard. But of course no rooinek can make a living out of farming, unless they send him money every month from England. And we found out that almost all the money Webber had was what he paid on the farm. He was always reading in those green books what he had to do. It's lucky that those books are written in English, and that the Boers can't read them. Otherwise many more farmers would be ruined every year. When his cattle had the heart-water, or his sheep had the blue-tongue, or there were cutworms or stalk-borers in his mealies, Webber would look it all up in his books. I suppose that when the kafirs stole his sheep he would look that up, too.

Still, Koos Steyn helped Webber quite a lot and taught him a number of things, so that matters did not go as badly with him as they would have if he had only acted according to the lies that were printed in those green books. Webber and Koos Steyn became very friendly. Koos Steyn's wife had had a baby just a few weeks before Webber came. It was the first child they had after being married seven years, and they were very proud of it. It was a girl. Koos Steyn said that he would sooner it had been a boy; but that, even so, it was better than nothing. Right from the first Webber had taken a liking to that child, who was christened Jemima after her mother. Often when I passed Koos Steyn's house I saw the Englishman sitting on the front stoep with the child on his knees.

In the meantime the other farmers around there became annoyed on account of Koos Steyn's friendship with the rooinek. They said that Koos was a handsupper and a traitor to his country. He was intimate with a man who had helped to bring about the downfall of the Afrikaner nation. Yet it was not fair to call Koos a handsupper. Koos had lived in the Graaff-Reinet District when the war broke out, so that he was a Cape Boer and need not have fought. Nevertheless, he joined up with a Free State commando and remained until peace was made, and if at any time the English caught him they would have shot him as a rebel, in the same way they shot Scheepers and many others.

Gerhardus Grobbelaar spoke about this once when we were in Willem Odendaal's post office.

"You are not doing right," Gerhardus said. "Boer and Englishman have been enemies since before Slagtersnek. We've lost this war, but some day we'll win. It's the duty we owe to our children's children to stand against the rooineks. Remember the concentration camps."

There seemed to me to be truth in what Gerhardus said.

"But the English are here now, and we've got to live with them," Koos answered. "When we get to understand one another perhaps we won't need to fight any more. This Englishman Webber is learning Afrikaans very well; and some day he might almost be one of us. The only thing I can't understand about him is that he has a bath every morning. But if he stops that and if he doesn't brush his teeth any more you will hardly be able to tell him from a Boer."

Although he made a joke about it, I felt that in what Koos Steyn said there was also truth.

Then, the year after the drought, the miltsiek broke out. The miltsiek seemed to be in the grass of the veld, and in the water of the dams, and even in the air the cattle breathed. All over the place I would find cows and oxen lying dead. We all became very discouraged. Nearly all of us in that part of the Marico had started farming again on what the Government had given us. Now that the stock died we had nothing. First the drought had put us back to where we were when we started. Now with the miltsiek we couldn't hope to do anything. We couldn't even sow mealies, because, at the rate at which the cattle were dying, in a short while we would have no oxen left to pull the plough. People talked of selling what they had and going to look for work on the gold mines. We sent a petition to the Government, but that did no good.

It was then that somebody got hold of the idea of trekking. In a few days we were talking of nothing else. But the question was where we could trek to. They would not allow us into Rhodesia for fear we might spread the miltsiek there as well. And it was useless going to any other part of the Transvaal. Somebody mentioned German West Africa. We had none of us been there before, and I suppose that really was the reason why, in the end, we decided to go there.

"The blight of the English is over South Africa," Gerhardus Grobbelaar said. "We'll remain here only to die. We must go away somewhere where there is not the Englishman's flag.

In a few weeks' time we arranged everything. We were going to trek across the Kalahari into German territory. Everything we had we loaded up. We drove the cattle ahead and followed behind on our wagons. There were five families: the Steyns, the Grobbelaars, the Odendaals, the Ferreiras and Sannie and I. Webber also came with us. I think it was not so much that he was anxious to leave as that he and Koos Steyn had become very much attached to one another, and the Englishman did not wish to remain alone behind.

The youngest person in our trek was Koos Steyn's daughter Jemima, who was then about eighteen months old. Being the baby, she was a favourite with all of us.

Webber sold his wagon and went with Koos Steyn's trek.

When at the end of the first day we outspanned several miles inside the Bechuanaland Protectorate, we were very pleased that we were done with the Transvaal, where we had had so much misfortune. Of course, the Protectorate was also British territory, but all the same we felt happier there than we had done in our country. We saw Webber every day now, and although he was a foreigner with strange ways, and would remain an Uitlander until he died, yet we disliked him less than before for being a rooinek.

It was on the first Sunday that we reached Malopolole. For the first part of our way the country remained Bushveld. There were the same kind of thorn-trees that grew in the Marico, except that they became fewer the deeper into the Kalahari that we went. Also, the ground became more and more sandy, until even before we came to Malopolole it was all desert. But scattered thorn-bushes remained all the way. That Sunday we held a religious service. Gerhardus Grobbelaar read a chapter out of the Bible and offered up a prayer. We sang a number of psalms, after which Gerhardus prayed again. I shall always remember that Sunday and the way we sat on the ground beside one of the wagons, listening to Gerhardus. That was the last Sunday that we were all together.

The Englishman sat next to Koos Steyn and the baby Jemima lay down in front of him. She played with Webber's fingers and tried to bite them. It was funny to watch her. Several times Webber looked down at her and smiled. I thought then that although Webber was not one of us, yet Jemima certainly did not know it. Maybe in a thing like that the child was wiser than we were. To her it made no difference that the man whose fingers she bit was born in another country and did not speak the same language that she did.

There are many things that I remember about that trek into the Kalahari. But one thing that now seems strange to me is the way in which, right from the first day, we took Gerhardus Grobbelaar for our leader. Whatever he said we just seemed to do without talking very much about it. We all felt that it was right simply because Gerhardus wished it. That was a strange thing about our trek. It was not simply that we knew Gerhardus had got the Lord with him – for we did know that – but it was rather that we believed in Gerhardus as well as in the Lord. I think that even if Gerhardus Grobbelaar had been an ungodly man we would still have followed him in exactly the same way. For when you are in the desert and there is no water and the way back is long, then you feel that it is better to have with you a strong man who does not read the Book very much, than a man who is good and religious, and yet does not seem sure how far to trek each day and where to outspan.

But Gerhardus Grobbelaar was a man of God. At the same time there was something about him that made you feel that it was only by acting as he advised that you could succeed. There was only one other man I have ever known who found it so easy to get people to do as he wanted. And that was Paul Kruger. He was very much like Gerhardus Grobbelaar, except that Gerhardus was less quarrelsome. But of the two Paul Kruger was the bigger man.

Only once do I remember Gerhardus losing his temper. And that was with the Nagmaal at Elandsberg. It was on a Sunday and we were camped out beside the Crocodile River. Gerhardus went round early in the morning from wagon to wagon and told us that he wanted everybody to come over to where his wagon stood. The Lord had been good to us at that time, so that we had had much rain and our cattle were fat. Gerhardus explained that he wanted to hold a service, to thank the Lord for all His good works, but more especially for what He had done for the farmers on the northern part of the Groot Marico District. This was a good plan, and we all came together with our Bibles and hymn-books. But one man, Karel Pieterse, remained behind at his wagon. Twice Gerhardus went to call him, but Karel Pieterse lay down on the grass and would not get up to come to the service. He said it was all right thanking the Lord now that there had been rains, but what about all those seasons when there had been drought and the cattle had died of thirst. Gerhardus Grobbelaar shook his head sadly, and said there was nothing he could do then as it was Sunday. But he prayed that the Lord would soften Brother Pieterse's heart, and he finished off his prayer by saying that in any case, in the morning, he would help to soften the brother's heart himself.

The following morning Gerhardus walked over with a sjambok and an ox-riem to where Karel Pieterse sat before his fire, watching the kafir making coffee. They were both of them men who were big in the body. But Gerhardus got the better of the struggle. In the end he won. He fastened Karel to the wheel of his own wagon with the ox-riem. Then he thrashed him with the sjambok while Karel's wife and children were looking on.

That had happened years before. But nobody had forgotten. And now, in the Kalahari, when Gerhardus summoned us to a service, it was noticed that no man stayed away.

Just outside Malopolole is a muddy stream that is dry part of the year and part of the year has a foot or so of brackish water. We were lucky in being there just at the time when it had water. Early the following morning we filled up the water-barrels that we had put on our wagons before leaving Marico. We were going right into the desert, and we did not know where we would get water again. Even the Bakwena kafirs could not tell us for sure.

"The Great Dorstland Trek," Koos Steyn shouted as we got ready to move off. "Anyway, we won't fare as badly as the Dorstland Trekkers. We'll lose less cattle than they did because we've got less to lose. And seeing that we are only five families, not more than about a dozen of us will die of thirst."

I thought it was bad luck for Koos Steyn to make jokes like that about the Dorstland Trek, and I think that others felt the same about it. We trekked right through the day, and it was all desert. By sunset we had not come across a sign of water anywhere. Abraham Ferreira said towards evening that perhaps it would be better if we went back to Malopolole and tried to find out for sure which was the best way of getting through the Kalahari. But the rest said that there was no need to do that, since we would be sure to come across water the next day. And, anyway, we were

Doppers and, having once set out, we were not going to turn back. But after we had given the cattle water our barrels did not have too much left in them.

By the middle of the following day all our water had given out except a little that we kept for the children. But still we pushed on. Now that we had gone so far we were afraid to go back because of the long way that we would have to go without water to get back to Malopolole. In the evening we were very anxious. We all knelt down in the sand and prayed. Gerhardus Grobbelaar's voice sounded very deep and earnest when he besought God to have mercy on us, especially for the sakes of the little ones. He mentioned the baby Jemima by name.

It was moonlight. All around us was the desert. Our wagons seemed very small and lonely; there was something about them that looked very mournful. The women and the children put their arms round one another and wept a long while. Our kafirs stood some distance away and watched us. My wife Sannie put her hand in mine, and I thought of the concentration camp. Poor woman, she had suffered much. And I knew that her thoughts were the same as my own: that after all it was perhaps better that our children should have died then than now.

We had got so far into the desert that we began telling one another that we must be near the end. Although we knew that German West was far away, and that in the way we had been travelling we had got little more than into the beginning of the Kalahari, yet we tried to tell one another lies about how near water was likely to be. But, of course, we told those lies only to one another. Each man in his own heart knew what the real truth was. And later on we even stopped telling one another lies about what a good chance we had of getting out alive. You can understand how badly things had gone with us when you know that we no longer troubled about hiding our position from the women and children. They wept, some of them. But that made no difference then. Nobody tried to comfort the women and children who cried. We knew that tears were useless, and yet somehow at that hour we felt that the weeping of the women was not less useless than the courage of the men. After a while there was no more weeping in our camp. Some of the women who lived through the dreadful things of the days that came after, and got safely back to the

48

Transvaal, never again wept. What they had seen appeared to have hardened them. In this respect they had become as men. I think that is the saddest thing that ever happens in this world, when women pass through great suffering that makes them become as men.

That night we hardly slept. Early the next morning the men went out to look for water. An hour after sun-up Ferreira came back and told us that he had found a muddy pool a few miles away. We all went there, but there wasn't much water. Still, we got a little, and that made us feel better. It was only when it came to driving our cattle towards the mudhole that we found our kafirs had deserted us during the night. After we had gone to sleep they had stolen away. Some of the weaker cattle couldn't get up to go to the pool. So we left them. Some were trampled to death or got choked in the mud, and we had to pull them out to let the rest get to the hole. It was pitiful.

Just before we left one of Ferreira's daughters died. We scooped a hole in the sand and buried her.

So we decided to trek back.

After his daughter was dead Abraham Ferreira went up to Gerhardus and told him that if we had taken his advice earlier on and gone back, his daughter would not have died.

"Your daughter is dead now, Abraham," Gerhardus said. "It is no use talking about her any longer. We all have to die some day. I refused to go back earlier. I have decided to go back now."

Abraham Ferreira looked Gerhardus in the eyes and laughed. I shall always remember how that laughter sounded on the desert. In Abraham's voice there was the hoarseness of the sand and thirst. His voice was cracked with what the desert had done to him; his face was lined and his lips were blackened. But there was nothing about him that spoke of grief for his daughter's death.

"Your daughter is still alive, Oom Gerhardus," Abraham Ferreira said, pointing to the wagon wherein lay Gerhardus' wife, who was weak, and the child to whom she had given birth two years before. "Yes, she is still alive . . . so far."

Ferreira turned away laughing, and we heard him a little later explaining to his wife in cracked tones about the joke he had made.

Gerhardus Grobbelaar watched the other men walk away without saying anything. So far we had followed Gerhardus through all things, and our faith in him had been great. But now that he had decided to trek back we lost our belief in him. We lost it suddenly, too. We knew that it was best to turn back, and that to continue would mean that we would all die on the Kalahari. And yet, if Gerhardus had said we must still go on we would have done so. We would have gone through with him right to the end. But now that he as much as said he was beaten by the desert we had no more faith in Gerhardus. That is why I have said that Paul Kruger was a greater man than Gerhardus. Because Paul Kruger was that kind of man whom we still worshipped even when he decided to retreat. If it had been Paul Kruger who told us that we had to go back we would have returned with strong hearts. We would have retained exactly the same love for our leader, even if we knew that he was beaten. But from the moment that Gerhardus said we must go back we all knew that he was no longer our leader. Gerhardus knew that also.

We knew what lay between us and Malopolole and there was grave doubt in our hearts when we turned our wagons round. Our cattle were very weak, and we had to inspan all that could walk. We hadn't enough yokes, and therefore we cut poles from the scattered bushes and tied them to the trek chains. As we were also without skeis we had to fasten the necks of the oxen straight on to the yokes with strops, and several of the oxen got strangled.

Then we saw that Koos Steyn had become mad. For he refused to return. He inspanned his oxen and got ready to trek on. His wife sat silent in the wagon with the baby; wherever her husband went she would go, too. That was only right, of course. Some women kissed her good-bye and cried. But Koos Steyn's wife did not cry. We reasoned with Koos about it, but he said that he had made up his mind to cross the Kalahari, and he was not going to turn back for just nonsense.

"But, man," Gerhardus Grobbelaar said to him, "you've got no water to drink."

"I'll drink coffee then," Koos Steyn answered, laughing as always, and took up the whip and walked away beside the wagon. And Webber went off with him, just because Koos Steyn had been good to him, I suppose. That's why I have said that Englishmen are queer. Webber must have known that if Koos Steyn had not actually gone wrong in the head, still what he was doing now was madness, and yet he stayed with him.

We separated. Our wagons went slowly back to Malopolole. Koos Steyn's wagon went deeper into the desert. My wagon went last. I looked back at the Steyns. At that moment Webber also looked round. He saw me and waved his hand. It reminded me of that day in the Boer War when that other Englishman, whose companion we had shot, also turned round and waved.

Eventually we got back to Malopolole with two wagons and a handful of cattle. We abandoned the other wagons. Awful things happened on that desert. A number of children died. Gerhardus Grobbelaar's wagon was in front of me. Once I saw a bundle being dropped through the side of the wagon-tent. I knew what it was. Gerhardus would not trouble to bury his dead child, and his wife lay in the tent too weak to move. So I got off the wagon and scraped a small heap of sand over the body. All I remember of the rest of the journey to Malopolole is the sun and the sand. And the thirst. Although at one time we thought we had lost our way, yet that did not matter much to us. We were past feeling. We could neither pray nor curse, our parched tongues cleaving to the roofs of our mouths.

Until to-day I am not sure how many days we were on our way back, unless I sit down and work it all out, and then I suppose I get it wrong. We got back to Malopolole and water. We said we would never go away from there again. I don't think that even those parents who had lost children grieved about them then. They were stunned with what they had gone through. But I knew that later on it would all come back again. Then they would re-member things about shallow graves in the sand, and Gerhardus Grobbelaar and his wife would think of a little bundle lying out in the Kalahari. And I knew how they would feel.

Afterwards we fitted out a wagon with fresh oxen; we took an abundant supply of water and went back into the desert to look for the Steyn family. With the help of the Sechuana kafirs, who could see tracks that we could not see, we found the wagon. The oxen had been outspanned; a few lay dead beside the wagon. The kafirs pointed out to us footprints on the sand, which showed which way those two men and that woman had gone.

In the end we found them.

Koos Steyn and his wife lay side by side in the sand; the woman's head rested on the man's shoulder; her long hair had become loosened, and blew softly in the wind. A great deal of fine sand had drifted over their bodies. We never found the baby Jemima. She must have died somewhere along the way and Koos Steyn must have buried her. But we agreed that the Englishman Webber must have passed through terrible things; he could not even have had any understanding left as to what the Steyns had done with their baby. He probably thought, up to the moment when he died, that he was carrying the child. For, when we lifted his body, we found, still clasped in his dead and rigid arms, a few old rags and a child's clothes.

It seemed to us that the wind that always stirs in the Kalahari blew very quietly and softly that morning.

Yes, the wind blew very gently.

FROM *Cold Stone Jug* (1949)

A Chronicle: being the unimpassioned record of
a somewhat lengthy sojourn in prison.

"Murder," I Answered

There were about a dozen prisoners in the cells at Marshall Square. It was getting on towards the late afternoon on a Sunday that we had spent locked up in a cell that was three-quarters underground and that had barred apertures opening on to the pavement at the corner of McLaren and Marshall Streets, Johannesburg. I had been arrested about fifteen or sixteen hours before.

Those first hours in the cells at Marshall Square, serving as the overture to a long period of imprisonment in the Swartklei Great Prison, were the most miserable I have ever known. By standing on a bench you could get near enough to the barred opening to catch an occasional glimpse of passing pedestrians, who, on that dreary Sunday afternoon, consisted almost entirely of Natives. The motley collection of prisoners inside the cell took turns in getting on to the bench and trying to attract the attention of the passers-by. Now and again a Native would stop. A lengthy discussion would follow. Occasionally (this constituting a triumphant termination to the interview), a piece of lighted cigarette-end would be dropped in through that little hole in the wall against the pavement. This was over twenty years ago. But it is still like that. You can go and look there.

For the rest of the time the dozen inmates of the cell carried on a desultory conversation, a lot of it having to do with what appeared to be highly unbecoming activities on the part of the plainclothes members of the police force, who seemed to spend all their walking hours in working up spurious cases against law-abiding citizens. Then, when it was getting towards late afternoon, one of the prisoners, a dapper little fellow who had done most of the talking and who seemed to exercise some sort of leadership in the cell, felt that it was time we all got sort of cosy together, and started taking more of a personal interest in one another's affairs.

"I'm in for liquor-selling, myself," he announced to a man standing next to him. "What they pinched you for?"

"Stealing a wheel-barrow from the P.W.D.," was the reply. "Not that I done it, mind you. But that's the charge."

"And what are you in for?" the cell-boss demanded of the next man.

"Drunk and disorderly and indecent exposure," came the answer.

"And what's your charge?"

,"Forgery. And if I drop this time I'll get seven years."

And so this dapper little fellow who was doing the questioning worked his way through the whole lot until it came to my turn.

"Say, what are you pinched for?" he asked, eyeing me narrowly.

"Murder," I said. And in my tone there was no discourtesy. And I did not glower much. I only added, "And I'm not feeling too good."

"Struth!" my interrogator remarked. And his jaw dropped. And that bunch of prisoners in the cell, the whole dozen of them, moved right across to the other side, to the corner that was furthest away from me.

Mother's Day

It was a Sunday on which the Dutch Reformed Church was honouring the mothers of the country.

And for the mother's day service in the Swartklei Prison chapel the Predikant had brought along a large number of paper labels, coloured respectively green and purple. The labels were passed round. This was something new and exciting. It made all us convicts attending the Dutch Reformed service in the prison chapel feel important people, somehow. If your mother was still alive you were expected to fix a green strip of paper on to the lapel of your brown corduroy jacket. If your mother was dead you fastened on a purple strip. No pins were provided, but the backs of these strips of coloured paper were gummed. So we stuck the labels on with spit. And we sat there, on the wooden benches, straight up and very proud, feeling not only that we were doing homage to our mothers, but that we were participating in a ceremony that was on that day being observed in the magical world known as "outside".

"They are having mothers' day outside, also," one convict would say to another.

People in churches outside, men as well as women (the entrancing sound of the word "women"!) were wearing little labels like these on their breasts. We were just like *outside* for those minutes during which the service in the prison chapel lasted. And we relished that period to the full, basking in the pride of being, for a while, like people who were free to roam the streets. Able to do the same things that men and women who were not in prison were doing. Sharing in *their* emotions. Feeling about things the way *they* felt.

The Predikant spoke in a very moving way about our mothers, and about us, also, about those of us whose mothers were still alive and who accordingly were privileged to wear green labels, and about those of us who had unfortunately lost our mothers, and so wore purple labels in sorrowful remembrance. (The Predikant pointedly made no reference to those convicts in his congregation who, through ignorance or misguided zeal, had stuck whole rows of labels, purple and green mixed up just anyhow, on to their jackets, like they were military ribbons). The result was, what with the hymn-singing and all, that the convicts got worked up to such a pitch of emotionalism that even the most hardened blue-coats (habitual criminals) broke down and sobbed. Men who had spent many years in prison and had grown grey behind bars, looking at the pathetic strips of coloured paper stuck on to their lapels with spit, dissolved into tears.

When the service ended and we tramped down the iron stairs back to the cells (encountering the Methodists, who were coming up the stairs as we were going down) a blue-coat in front of me, his face still tearful after the sermon, inadvertently collided with a convict tramping up to attend the Methodist service.

"As jy my weer stamp, donder ek jou," the blue-coat said, but his tone was kindly. The thought of the way he had been breaking his mother's heart through the years had softened him. His language, through long habit, held low menace. But his ton was unexpectedly mild.

Death Cell

Now for the murderers. Compared with the blue-coats, they are rather a jolly lot. The majority of them are first offenders. This is not surprising, of course. Murder being the crime it is, it is unlikely that anybody will feel like committing it a number of times. For that matter, you're not allowed to commit murder a number of times . . . The result is that by far the majority of murderers doing stretches in the Swartklei Great Prison are first offenders. A murderer never comes back to prison, either. It is almost as though murder, the capital crime, is the only one that appeals to him. The other offences under common law seem too tame, by comparison, to be able to tempt him. The murderer is a strange figure; not pathetic, like the blue-coat; but lonely somehow: almost like the eagle. But also with the lost bewilderment of a child.

In prison, the murderer, unlike the blue-coat, does not wear a distinctive garb. He is not dressed by the authorities in a way to single him out from the other convicts – bank-robbers, forgers, illicit gold-buyers, rapists and the rest. There is no need for men to put any distinguishing marks on a murderer's clothes. Cain's mark is there for all to read. Murder is a doomed sign to wear on your brow.

Disguise it how one will, the fact is that the Swartklei Great Prison is dominated, spiritually as well as architecturally, by the gallows chamber, whose doors rise up, massive and forbidding, at the end of the main wing in the building – the penal corridors.

The hangings are the worst part of life inside the prison. When a man has been condemned to death on the Rand or in any other Transvaal centre he is brought over to the Swartklei Great Prison, where he is lodged in the condemned cell adjacent to the gallows until such time as he is either reprieved or hanged. The period of waiting in that cell next to the gallows varies from about five weeks to two months. Then the case is settled one way or another. Either the sheriff arrives with a printed document bearing the title "Greetings" in heavy black scroll and he notifies the condemned man that his execution has been set down for the morning after the next, or the Governor of the prison walks in, accompanied by the chief warder, and he informs the prisoner that the Governor-General has decided to commute his sentence to one of imprisonment, the term varying usually from ten years to life.

But during all this time the shadow of this hanging lies like a pall over the inmates of the prison, warders as well as convicts. During most of the months of the year the condemned cells are empty. There is nobody waiting up there at the end of the penal section with the death sentence suspended over him. But when the condemned cells are occupied, things in the prison are rotten all round. There is something inside the most hardened warder or anti-social convict that makes him shudder at the thought of death, of violent death, of the gruesome ceremony of doing a man to death above a dark hole, at a set time, with legal formality that does not extend beyond hand-cuffs and leg-irons and a sack drawn over the condemned man's head and a piece of coarse rope knotted behind his ear.

On the morning of a hanging the cells are unlocked half an hour later than usual. The prisoners arrive at their workshops half an hour late. The cells are all locked at the hour of the hanging and the morning bell doesn't ring until the execution is over. The man in the condemned cell must not be allowed to know how near his hour has actually come. They say it is all done very efficiently. They say that it takes less than two minutes from the moment the hangman has unlocked the door of the condemned cell until he has got the prisoner trussed and pinioned and with the rope round his neck, waiting for the trap-door to fall. When the trap drops it is with a reverberation that shakes the whole prison building, and the bell rings, and the cells are unlocked and the convicts march out to work.

I dislike according so much space to the details of hanging, but these things loom like a shadow over the prison all the time, like an unpleasant odour, and they make life inside the prison a lot gloomier than it would otherwise be. The six hundred convicts and the hundred warders in the prison share to some extent the feelings of the man who is being dropped through the trap-door, and the fountain-head of life grows discoloured. I don't suppose very much can be done about it. After all, prison isn't supposed to be a place where you can just spend a few happy, carefree years at will.

I remember that I had company in the condemned cell. There was another man there, also under sentence of death, when I arrived. We were separated from each other by two rows of bars and wire netting, which formed a little passage in which the warder on duty paced up and down. The warders watched us night and day, working in four-hour shifts, with the lights on all the time. That other man's name was Stoffels. We were provided with cigarettes, which the warder would light for us through the wire-netting. I remember the smell of disinfectant in that cell. It is a kind of disinfectant that they use in a number of Government institutions. The smell is strong but not unpleasant. Only the other day I got a whiff of this same disinfectant in a post office corridor. And in one punch that odour brought the past back to me like it was now. I even looked round to see whether the sanitary pail was still there, in the corner.

But I can recall only the external impressions, the surface things, which I have learnt are not realities at all.

I can remember the jokes Stoffels and I made, talking to each other through two sets of steel netting and bars, with the warder in between. And the questions we asked the warders about life inside the prison. We had to ask these questions of the warders, we two, who were in the prison but not of it. And the stories the warders had to relate to us, in the long nights when we couldn't get to sleep, made life as a convict inside a prison seem very alluring – just simply because it was life. And when we heard the convicts march out to work in the mornings, their footsteps heavy on the concrete floor of the hall far removed from us, their passage sounded like the tread of kings. And when a warder mentioned to us the fact that he had that morning had occasion, in the course of an altercation, to hit a convict over the head with his baton, I know how I felt about that convict, how I envied him, how infinitely privileged I felt he was to be able to be regarded by a warder as a live person, as somebody that could be hit over the head.

For no warder would dream of hitting a condemned man with a baton. To a warder a condemned man was something already dead.

Because we had been sentenced to be hanged, Stoffels. and I were accorded certain privileges. For one thing, we didn't have to get our hair cropped short, like the other convicts, with a pair of number nought clippers. And when I was taken out on exercise, into the prison yard, twice a day, and I saw other convicts from a distance, and I saw how short their hair was, and I felt my own hair, long and wavy, and I understood what my long hair signified – then I didn't feel too good. I even hoped that, somehow, by mistake, somebody would come in and say that the chief warder had ordered my hair to be cut short. Just so I wouldn't have to flaunt, in the exercise yard, that awful thing that made me different from the hard-labour convicts. Long hair and the rope . . . A short rope.

Of course, Stoffels and I affected unconcern there in the condemned cell. We spent much of our waking hours in pulling the warders' legs. We didn't know, then, that we were in actual fact engaged in a time-honoured prison pastime. We didn't know that "kidding" the warders was a sport regularly indulged in by prison lags, and that this form of recreation had venerable traditions. We didn't know all that. We merely followed our natural bent of trying to be funny, and we found, afterwards, that we were all the time conforming to accepted prison custom. It must be that prison was, after all, the right place for Stoffels and me. Because to this aspect of it, at all events, to the part of it connected with pulling a warder's leg, we took like ducks to water.

There was one warder whom Stoffels and I nicknamed the Clown. He had not been in the prison service very long and had only recently been transferred to the Swartklei Great Prison from a native gaol in Barberton. We joshed him unmercifully. He was a young fellow in his early twenties, but Stoffels and I addressed him as though he were a man of the world with infinitely wide experience and an oracle of learning. He afforded us many nights of first-class entertainment, during the dreary hours between ten at night and two in the morning, when we could not sleep and were afraid to trust our head to the hard pallet, in case when we woke up in the morning it would be to find the sheriff standing at the door, with the death-warrant.

The Clown had a very simple heart. One night, through a process of not very subtle flattery, we got him to acknowledge that he could dance rather well. We also got him to admit that, in general, men were envious of his ballroom accomplishments, and that, behind his back, they said many nasty things about him, such as that he danced like a sick hippopotamus, or the way a duck waddles. All because they were jealous of him. We even got him so far as to show us a few of the latest dance-steps. For this purpose he took off his heavy warder's boots. At the Clown's demonstration, in his stockinged feet, of the then-fashionable black-bottom, Stoffels and I laughed uproariously. We explained to him, of course, that we were laughing at the thought that jealous males could have come to such ludicrously erroneous conclusions about his dancing, merely because they viewed everything he did through the green gaze of envy. Thereupon the Clown joined in the laughter, thus making Stoffels and me roar louder than ever.

"Didn't they perhaps, in their jealousy, even say . . ." I started off again when we all suddenly stopped laughing. For a key grated in the outer door and the night head-warder entered.

"What's all this?" he demanded. "The convicts the other end of the hall are complaining they can't sleep, the way you men in the condemned cell keep on laughing all night. And this isn't the first night, neither."

The night head-warder looked at us sternly. There seemed something gravely irregular in a situation in which two condemned men were keeping a whole prison establishment awake with indecorous laughter.

"You condemned men mustn't laugh so loud," he said. "The hard labour convicts got to sleep. They got to work all day. You two don't do nothing but smoke cigarettes all day long and crack jokes. You'll get yourselves in serious trouble if the Governor finds out you keep the whole prison awake night after night, romping about and laughing in the condemned cells."

I wondered, vaguely, what more serious trouble we could get into than we were already in. But at that moment the night-warder happened to look down at the Clown's feet. So it was his turn to laugh. The Clown certainly cut a ridiculous figure, with shapeless pieces of feet leaking out of his socks.

"Where's your boots?" the night-warder demanded, his tone between a threat and a guffaw. "Don't you know as you can't come on duty improperly dressed? What sort of a example do you think you are to these two condemned men? And look at all them pertaters in your socks. I never seen so many pertaters in a sock. More pertater than sock. With all them pertaters you ought to be working in the kitchen. Come on, now. Quick about it. Put on the other boot, too. What you want to take them off for, anyway? To show these condemned men your pertaters, I suppose. Or maybe you got bunions. Yes, must be bunions. I suppose you got bunions on your feet through walking about the streets looking for trollops."

With that sally, and still guffawing, the night head-warder departed. There certainly seemed to be something in the atmosphere of the cell adjacent to the gallows that was provocative of a spirit of clean fun. The condemned cell air seemed to be infectiously mirth-making.

"Now, isn't that just what we have been saying?" Stoffels asked of the Clown when the three of us were alone together, once more. "How do you like that for jealousy? The moment the night head-warder sees you he starts picking you out. What do you think of that? And so ridiculous, too. How can he say you got those bunions on your feet . . ."

"But I haven't got bunions," the Clown asserted, "You know as well as I do that I took off my boots to show my . . ."

"Those terrible bunions," Stoffels persisted, ignoring the Clown's remonstrances. "How can he say you got those corns and bunions and blisters walking after whores in the street? Has he ever seen you walking after a whore in the street? Come on, answer me, has he ever seen you?"

"I don't know what he's seen or what he hasn't seen," the Clown answered. "I only know that the only times I've ever walked about looking for a whore it was in the other end of the town from where he stays. It was . . ."

Reprieve

I don't want to waste any more time writing about the condemned cell. I want to get on with the next part of the story. In fact, I want to get out of the condemned cell as quick as possible. As quick as I got out of it that afternoon when the Governor came up and informed me that I had been reprieved. I was asleep on my blankets on the floor, that afternoon. I was dreaming, but I forget what about. And I awoke to find the Governor and the chief warder and the section officer and the warder on duty in the death cell, all together standing in a ring around me. I woke up and rubbed my eyes. The Governor was talking. And on a sudden the import of his words and his visit dawned on me. It was the Governor who had called on me, and not the sheriff. Not the sheriff. Then I got the gist of it. The Governor was saying that my sentence had been commuted to a term of imprisonment with hard labour for so many years. I got out of that condemned cell in such a hurry that I didn't hear all the years. And afterwards when I did find out (because they took me down into the hall later on and got the number of years written on my ticket) that knowledge did not sober me up.

On the way down the hall the head-warder addressed me in terms of stern admonition.

"You're a bleeding hard-labour – convict now," he said. "See? And we don't want none of your – sanguinary cheek here. You broke your – mother's heart and we'll break your – heart. We tame lions here. First peep out of you, my man, and I'll see you get six days' solitary on spare diet. Pick up your step, there! You're not a blooming condemn' cell favourite no longer. You'll be – sorry it wasn't the hangman by the time we finished with you. You'll find out – double quick there's no blasted favouritism here."

"Yes, Sir," I answered the head-warder and followed a discipline-warder across the length of the hall and then in through a grille gate and then up a flight of iron stairs that brought me on a landing consisting of two sets of cages. They were steel cages, partitioned from each other by bolted steel plates, like you see in a ship. One row has steel plates in front as well; the other row had bars and wire mesh. I hoped they would put me in a cage with bars and wire mesh in front. You could see a little way out into the passage through the wire. And the all-steel cage looked somewhat cold. But my luck was out. The section-warder took me along a passage, unlocked an all-steel cage, waited for me to enter and then without a word, slammed the steel door shut on me; and left.

I found out, when we were next unlocked, that I was in A-2 Section, the first-offenders' section, and that long-timers were kept in the all-steel cages and only short-timers were allowed in the cages with wire-fronts.

In that cage in A-2 Section I spent quite a number of years.

Printshop

After a couple of years the job of building the wall and the work-shops was ended, and we in the stone-yard returned to our old routine of sitting down in long rows, chopping stones into small bits. But, like my sojourn in the printers' shop, the experience I acquired of the building trade also stood me in good stead in later years. The knack of tipping a loaded wheelbarrow is always a useful accomplishment in life.

It took us a couple of years to build the wall and the workshops. A couple of years is all right, if you say it fast. But in prison it seems a long time. Even a short stretch seems to take a long time to do.

And talking about time, the doing it and the length of it, reminds me of what once happened in the printers' shop. The head-warder had discovered a whole lot of loose type under the floorboards. How the type got there was in this way : through the years, whenever a convict had a job of dissing to do that bored him, he would just take a column of type and drop it through a hole in the floor, thereby.saving himself the job of distributing all that stuff, letter by letter, into the various boxes. By the time the head-warder discovered that hole in the floor there was quite a mound of type lying there. The convicts all professed great interest and astonishment, averring their disapproval of the kind of person, lower than a rattlesnake's anus, who could chuck a lot of type under the floorboards in order to save himself a bit of extra work. That sort of thing never happened in their time, they declared. It must have happened in the old days, when those Australians were in the prison, and the convicts did not have the same sense of responsibility and honour and rectitude that animated them to-day.

Anyway, the head-warder had the floorboards torn up, and all the type was brought up from underneath, and it was all dumped into a huge box. To a convict named Botha was delegated the task of sorting all that vast chaos of type, letter by letter, into the various partitions in the type-cases. A corner in the printers' shop was specially fitted out for him. In the midst of many rows of cases, with the box full of assorted type of every variety of size and face before him, Botha would sit on a little stool, patiently picking out and distributing letters that varied from about 36-point Gill Sans Bold to 6-point italic and 10-point Doric.

"How long do you reckon the job will take you?" I asked of Botha, one day.

"About seven years," he replied.

His answer frightened me a little. I thought of a man outside. What doesn't happen to a man outside the prison in the course of seven years? The good years and the bad years. The adventures that come his way. The triumphs and the heartbreaks that are bound up with seven years of living. The processions of the seasons, spring succeeding winter and autumn following summer, seven times. A man could meet a girl and fall in love and get married and have quite a number of children in seven years. And he could get a job and get fired, and travel all over the world, and starve and succeed, and lust and weep and hate and take vengeance. All these things in all these years.

And during this time Botha the convict would be sorting the type out of the box. Only after seven years would his fingers close around the last pica space. And nothing would be happening to Botha during these years. Just nothing at all.

Another rather interesting thing happened in the printers' shop near the end of my stay there, just shortly before I was kicked out into the stone-yard. A warder named Marman, who was stationed at the local gaol, came into the printers' shop to relieve the printers' trades head-warder when he went on a month's leave. Now, the warder Marman had literary leanings. He had written a novel about prison life. He called the novel *Die Liefdesgeskiedenis van Bloubaadjie Theron.* The hero was a blue-coat. And discipline-warder Marman made a very noble figure out of him. He had been innocently convicted, quite a number of times, this blue-coat hero of Marman's romance, and he had never squealed, always taking the blame for what his friends or relatives did. But there was a girl who waited for this blue-coat through the years . . .

Anyway, it was a very moving story that this warder Marman wrote. It was full of slush and sentiment and melodrama and bad grammar. And he got us to print that book for him. He gave us a tin of tobacco apiece, and we worked like fury to be able to set and run off that little book, *Die Liefdesgeskiedenis van Bloubaadjie Theron*, before the trades head-warder came back from his leave. Four comps did the setting all by hand. I read the proofs. The machinemen made up and ran off each section as it was set. The cleaner washed the ink off the formes with soft soap each time a run was completed. And discipline-warder Marman kept watch at the door for the chief warder or the Governor, and he would say, "All correct, sir," when one of these superior officials happened along, and so nobody was the wiser. It was, I suppose, one of the biggest under-the-lap jobs ever undertaken in the prison.

About two days before the trades head-warder was due to return from leave the job was finished. The book looked quite imposing, although the sections weren't bound, but only stitched together with wire, and with paper covers. Marman took delivery, smuggling the books out under his raincoat, a few parcels at a time. And then we remembered something. Funny we hadn't thought of it before. There were many pages of this book still standing in type. The letters hadn't been distributed into the cases. It had been all right with the chief warder, and the other warder of the dicipline staff, who wouldn't know what was going on in the printers' shop in any case. But the moment the trades head-warder came back he would see all those pages set up in type and we would be exposed. The whole shop would be guilty. We worked like in a frenzy, dumping all that type back, letter by letter, into the various cases. But we still couldn't manage. We started chucking the letters in just anyhow, pie-ing the cases. But it was still no good. The head-warder would come back and find out what we had been up to.

Of course, there was no other solution, in the end. The floorboards which had been carefully nailed down after the type accumulated over the years had been retrieved and given to Botha to sort, were now prised up, once more. And the remaining chapters of discipline-warder Marman's novel, in the form of column after column of loose type set by hand, were shot through the hole in the floor.

By the time the trades head-warder returned the floor-boards were nailed down again, very neatly.

Food Strike

There was a time in the prison when the food was very bad.

First it was the bread. Then the mealie-pap got bad. Afterwards you couldn't eat the carrot soup either. The convicts expressed their disapproval in various ways. A few minor assaults were committed on some of the convicts working in the kitchen, when they brought the food into the hall on little trolleys. It didn't seem a particularly sensible sort of thing to do, assaulting the kitchen hands. The trouble seemed to have originated much higher up. Hitting a trolley-pushing convict from the kitchen over the head with a lump of iron – specially smuggled in from the workshops for that purpose – did not achieve very much in the way of improving the quality of the fare supplied three times a day to six hundred convicts. What was more, when these trifling assaults on the kitchen-hands grew in number, the chief warder made other arrangements about transporting the meals from the kitchen into the sections: he gave instructions that half-a-dozen members from the refuse-gang had to perform that office. It is a tribute to the good sense of the convicts that I am able to record the fact that only on two occasions were refuse-span convicts offered physical violence when pushing the food-trolleys into the hall.

But on each occasion you could smell, a long distance off, how bad the food was that was coming through the kitchen.

And there was just about nothing that we could do about it. Every lunch-time at least two dozen convicts would line up in the hall and, as an empty gesture, proclaim to the head warder that a dog couldn't eat porridge like that. Or that the beans weren't fit for pigs. Or that an orang-outang couldn't drink that soup.

But we couldn't get much satisfaction that way. Because the fault lay with people higher up than the kitchen. Maybe higher than the stores department, even. To try and remedy the matter by means of a daily gentlemanly protest – a couple of dozen of convicts gathering in the hall and showing the head warder the contents of their dixies – was just about as futile a procedure as taking an impatient kick at one of the trolley-wheels.

A convict would say to the head warder, "This isn't fit for a pig. Just taste it, sir."

Or another convict – equally unconscious of any innuendo – would say, "Just have a mouthful of this, sir. And tell us if you think a gorilla could swallow it."

Every time, of course, the head-warder would decline the proffered delicacy, on the pretext either that he had lunched, or that his wife was keeping lunch waiting for him, and if he ate now he wouldn't have any appetite for his food when he got home. Sometimes he simply said, straight out, that he wasn't hungry.

The only way to get better food was to demonstrate on a scale big enough to cause repercussions. Because the only satisfaction we got out of the head-warder was that he spoke severely to a number of the refuse-span convicts pushing the food-trolleys along.

"Aren't you ashamed to bring in muck like this?" he would ask these convicts who looked pretty sheepish, in any case, having to do this extra (and slightly risky) chore.

If the warder was in a bad mood, he would wax sarcastic.

"Of course, you convicts are used to only the best when you are outside," he would say. "Of course, you are used to having skoff in only the best hotels, where you tip the waiter ten bob and he polishes your top-hats on his sleeve. And through a miscarriage of the law you're all here behind bars and missing your champagne and caviare and Havanas. Perhaps I'll get my wife to cook some invalid soup for you big, strapping hoboes. And I'll smuggle the soup inside in a wash-tub hid under my tunic."

And we'd think, yes, we'd like to know what he hasn't in his time already smuggled into – and out of – the prison.

But we didn't say what we thought, of course, and the head-warder wouldn't say much more, either, except that at the end of his little speech he would remark, "Now beat it, you bums."

But when he was in a really bad humour, the head-warder would get threatening, and he would say, "Now, you get to hell out of it, the whole two dozen of you. Or I'll charge you before the Governor for making frivolous complaints."

72

And there were those among the convicts who said that he would charge them, also. But he would have to write out a charge-sheet, and he would have to fill in the nature of the charge he was bringing. And the head-warder didn't know how to spell *frivolous,* the convicts said. But this was another thing that they didn't say to his face, either.

Looking at that head-warder, I would wonder, idly, sometimes, as to how exactly he would spell the word *frivolous.* In a highly frivolous way, no doubt.

The upshot of it was that there were a few demonstrations. I would hardly say that these demonstrations were well-organised. The convicts did a number of spontaneously imitative things. One morning, for instance, all the portions of bread were flung into the hall. First one convict, standing on an upstairs landing overlooking the hall, pushed his bread through the bars and flung it down on to the floor below. Then another convict followed his example. In a few moments dozens of convicts were doing the same thing, pieces of soggy bread flying about the hall and landing on the head-warder's desk and messing up the floor, and landing near the head-warder, too, some of the bits. There was a terrific crush on the balconies at the end of the sections overlooking the hall, every convict dutifully bringing along his portion of bread and thrusting it through between the bars and sending it flying down into the hall. But it wasn't so much a sense of loyalty, perhaps, that animated the convicts in their participation in this gesture of convict-solidarity over the food question. It was just that it was fun to be able to commit an outrage like this, when there was something sort of sacrosanct about the hall, and it was jolly to be able to be defiant like that, just for once, putting your hand through between the bars and chucking your piece of bread down into the hall – with the prospect of even getting the head-warder on the head with it.

It was a nice feeling. "Yah – !" Like that. Cocking a snook at the whole prison. Tearing a sheet off the copy of the Prison Regulations and rolling a dagga-smoke in it. It gave you a wonderful sense of pure and heroic freedom, watching your own piece of bread landing in the hall, down below. But now I come to think of it, it seems that it wasn't such an unreasonable thing to do with that bread. You certainly couldn't eat it.

And the head-warder in the hall was in a very good mood that day. He didn't turn a hair.

"Waste not, want not, boys," was all he said, by way of admonition.

Nevertheless, it was a pretty sizable demonstration. On the way out from the sections and in the workshops the convicts naturally talked of nothing else.

"It was Alec the Ponce wot chucked in the first piece of bread," one convict said.

"It wasn't. It was Blue-coat Verdamp. I was standing as far off him as I am from you. And I chucked my bread in next, right after him. It was . . ."

"The first man that dumped his bread was a first offender. It come right down from the first offenders' section," somebody else said.

"Then it must have flew right back again," somebody interrupted him. "It couldn't come from the first offenders. The first offenders is all a lot of yellow rats, afraid to do a thing in case they loses their remission."

There were quite a number of fights in the stone-yard, that morning. It was a thorny issue. Who was to get the credit for having thought out and taken the lead in that startlingly original demonstration? It was an historical event. You ought to have seen how the hall looked. Nowhere to walk at all. Just bread all over the place. One of the convicts even swore that he saw a few bread-crumbs sticking behind the head-warder's ear, when he came close up to him. But somebody else said those crumbs were probably there from when the head-warder had breakfast, and that he had forgotten to wipe his face.

This was typical of the sort of opinions that prevailed among the prisoners about the head-warder.

But the question as to which was the convict that should get the honour for having taken the initiative in chucking his piece of bread into the hall was hedged around with all sorts of difficulties. Eventually, all the other claimants having been eliminated, it was agreed that it was either Alec the Ponce or Blue-coat Verdamp that had taken the lead. And by lunch-time it was pretty generally conceded that right was right, and that whatever views you held about Alec the Ponce, it was nevertheless a fact that he had chucked his bread into the hall at least two seconds before Blue-coat Verdamp had done so.

But there were supporters of Blue-coat Verdamp who maintained, in spite of all arguments and threats, that Blue-coat Verdamp had in actual fact got in first. When he saw the way public opinion was going, Blue-coat Verdamp got sore. He couldn't understand what was wrong with the boys, he declared. He had been in prison, on and off, from the very early days. In twenty years he had spent only two Christmases outside, he said. And the boys in the game were not what they used to be.

"Alec the Ponce is only doing four and a half years, ain't he?" the Blue-coat demanded truculently. "And I am doing twice as long as him, ain't I? And what's the blasted idea giving a short-timer, what's doing only four and a half years, credit over a long-timer like me? I got a good mind to go back into that hall and bring back my piece of bread."

Blue-coat Verdamp paused for a moment, then added savagely, "And eat it."

But his friends advised him not to do anything foolish. It would, of course, make Alec the Ponce and his supporters look very silly if Blue-coat Verdamp went back and took back his bread and ate it.

"But you'll get very sick, man, from that bread," somebody said. "Nobody can eat that bread and not go to hospital. Not even a head-warder can eat that bread."

"And how amongst all that bread will you find your own piece?" another man asked. "For all you know, you might even pick up Alec the Ponce's piece of bread, and eat it. And how will you feel then?"

It had been quite a good demonstration, throwing the bread into the hall like that. It was a pity that what had been an historic act should have left this aftermath of bitter dissension.

Now, there are a number of rather queer things about mob psychology. And I learnt one or two somewhat singular things during the course of the food-trouble, that McDougal seems to have left out of his text-book on psychology. For instance, after the first spontaneous expression of dissatisfaction in the form of the whole prison, including the first offenders' section, flinging its bread into the hall, nobody after that felt any kind of mass urge to repeat that particular kind of performance. The mass mind felt, instinctively, that future protests had to take some other form. But there were individuals, inside of this crowd of six hundred convicts, who hadn't the psychological sense to grasp this artistic truth. That was where men with the gift of leadership, like Blue-coat Verdamp and Alec the Ponce, knew their potatoes. But there were other convicts who hadn't this subtle, intuitive feeling about mob urges. One of these less highly-gifted persons was a first-offender named Winslow who had been a book-keeper in civilian life and who was now serving a sentence of three years for fraud.

It was Winslow's weakness that he was trying in and out of season, to set up as a prison-head. He would always be first with a new rumour. When there was talk, on the occasion of some event or other of national importance, about the remission of sentence that every convict would be sure to get, then Winslow would always be the first to impart, with a very knowing sort of air, exact information as to the form that the Governor-General's clemency was going to take. And events nearly always proved him wrong. Never mind anything else, almost every time when he thought we were going to have our sentences mitigated, it turned out that we got nothing off at all. The authorities never even thought of the prison. And so with everything else. When a new convict arrived, Winslow would always take him in tow, and teach him the ropes, so as to be able to pose to this new convict that he, Winslow, was a very big and important "head" who had decided to instruct a raw new-comer in the majestic lore of a great prison, merely because he was sorry for him. But after a week or two this greenhorn first-timer would learn enough of the ropes himself to cut out Winslow, who would then again be left friendless for a while, walking up and down the exercise yard on his own.

And when there was a concert, some party of amateur singers and guitar-players from head-office entertaining the convicts for an evening, then it would always be Winslow that tried to jump up first to make the customary little speech, thanking the visitors for having come round. Naturally, this effrontery on the part of a first offender annoyed those of the old hands who had come to regard this office, of making a little speech of thanks to the concert parties, as one of the privileges appertaining to certain select spirits who had served at least seven or eight sentences and had grown grey, so to speak, in the service of the prison. The result was that after he had been struck down one night, just after he had jumped to his feet and had got as far as "Mr. Governor and . . .", Winslow didn't try to make any more speeches in the hall. He was struck down with a lavatory seat specially torn from its hinges, earlier that afternoon, by some of the blue-coats in the penal section.

Incidentally, I have often wondered, since then, what the concert party thought of that little incident. There was a banjo-player, and a man who sang deep bass songs, and an amateur magician who juggled with cards (he had a nerve, all right: there were a number of cardsharpers among those six hundred convicts who could have shown him a trick or two, and not just platform tricks, but grim, real-life stuff) and half a dozen gentlemen who did not perform, but only sat back on the stage with their arms folded, very conscious of the fact that they were Distinguished Visitors, and that they would never land behind prison-bars, of course, and a man who blew on a trumpet, and some other men who sang, but not in such deep bass tones as the first one, and a man who told funny stories. They were stories that had been told often in the prison, and for that reason they were popular stories. The convicts knew exactly when the funny part was coming, and what the point of it was, and where to laugh, which they did, each time, uproariously. No humorous stories were as popular as the well-tried chestnuts. There was one story about a coloured girl called "Wi'lets" that brought the house down, regularly, year after year. And sometimes, when the humorist omitted to tell it, because he was already sick of it, no doubt, there would be a chorus of "Wi'lets" from hundreds of convict throats (and from the throats of quite a number of warders, too), so that this amateur public entertainer from the head-office would be constrained to relate this same little anecdote about "Wi'lets", in the same words and the same intonation that he had employed year after year for upward of a decade. And next morning, on their way out to the workshops, convicts would greet each other with this catchword, old crony calling to crony, "Wi'lets", even while they were still marching in line, and warders who were recruits would stare in amazement, but the old hands among the warders would smile indulgently.

The bass singer rendered the same solos, too, year after year. He was, as an entertainer, second in popularity only to the raconteur. The bass vocalist sang one thing that was a noble blending of the martial with the sentimental. It was a song about an old chateau, or an old chapeau, or an old shako: nobody ever caught that word properly. And it had a powerful refrain about "Ten, twenty, thirty – *forty* – years ago." It was a lovely song. And justly popular. The convicts thought that the "ten, twenty, thirty, *forty* years ago" had reference to the date when they were last outside, and they regarded the bass singer's regular inclusion of this item in his repertoire as a graceful gesture to the long-timers.

But to return to the last occasion on which Winslow jumped up and tried to thank the concert-party. I often wondered what those gentlemen from the Department of Justice head office in the Union Buildings thought, then, when the leader of the concert-party announced that there were no further items on the programme, and one of the convicts jumped up and began a little speech with the words "Mr. Governor and . . ." and then suddenly a lavatory-seat swung in a wide arc made contact with the top of his head, and he subsided without another word and had to be carried feet first back into the section, while a blue-coat, almost as though by arrangement, got up and made a sonorous, old-time sort of a speech, filled with battered clichés and good feeling and bad grammar, and expressing disappointment at the fact that the authorities had not seen fit to celebrate the successful combating of the locust plague in the Kalahari, last year, by granting some remission of sentence to the long-timers.

I suppose those gentlemen from head office, when they heard that speech and saw the lavatory-seat, and all – I suppose they just thought to themselves, "Ah, well."

No action was taken by the prison authorities against the convicts who had laid Winslow out at the concert. The warders weren't keen on a man like Winslow getting up and talking when officials from the Department of Justice were present. Not too well-educated themselves, they resented the idea that a man with some smatterings of learning should profess to represent the convicts. That wouldn't do. Where would the warders be if the idea got about in the Department of Justice that the men doing time in the prison were suave and polished and scholarly, and that the warders were a set of illiterate thugs? The warders were most happy when an after-the-concert speech was made by some stupid-looking blue-coat who drooled away for about five minutes in an incoherent form of prison slang, making homely references to his work in the mat-shop and to dietary matters.

Anyway, to return to the food disturbances . . . Winslow was out of touch with public opinion in the prison. He had but little intuition about the way people thought and felt *en masse*. So the next morning after the incident of the bread-throwing he made rather a fool of himself. Because the credit for having flung the first piece of bread into the hall was being shared between Alex the Ponce and Blue-coat Verdamp, these two men being thereby elevated to a position of high consequence in the life of the prison, Winslow felt that here was his chance to establish himself as leader of the first offenders' section. To-day he would be the first to fling his bread into the hall. The rest of the prison would pattern after him. He would be in the limelight.

Consequently, the moment his cell-door was unlocked, Winslow dashed out with his piece of bread and made for the landing. He got there before anybody else. He couldn't sense that there was no mass feeling in favour of repeating the demonstration of the day before. And he threw his bread right into the middle of the hall. And nobody followed his example. The head-warder was in the hall, seated at his desk. He was quite unperturbed at Winslow's action. The head-warder knew the psychology of the convicts much better than Winslow did. The head-warder rose from behind his desk, very slowly, fixed his eye on Winslow, who was standing on the first offenders' landing, his arm still extended from having propelled the bread through the bars, and beckoned to Winslow with one finger. That was all. The head-warder didn't talk. He knew he had his man dead to rights.

Like someone hypnotised, Winslow followed the head-warder's beckoning finger; he came down from the landing and descended the iron stairs and made his way down to the grille gate leading into the hall. The head-warder unlocked the grille gate for Winslow, took his ticket off him, and had him charged before the Governor. It was all done very neatly, and without commotion. And Winslow got about two weeks' solitary confinement on rice water. If it had not been for the exceptional circumstances prevailing in the prison, the Governor said, he would have given Winslow lashes. And the convicts said they were glad that Winslow had been dealt with.

And the old lags, with lots of previous convictions, said that the first offenders were getting more cheeky every day.

Nevertheless, for the next week or so, the food in the prison did show some sort of improvement.

And no more bread was cast into the hall thereafter. This wasn't so much on account of the fact that the convicts were supplied with more edible bread, but through a thoughtful step taken by the prison authorities. Many hundreds of square yards of steel-netting were ordered. All the convicts working in the fitters' and carpenters' shops were put on the job. And in next to no time the whole hall was closed in with steel-netting that you couldn't throw even mealie-porridge through.

The improvement in the quality of the food was as temporary as it was slight. Regularly, at meal-times, a couple of dozen convicts would again be lined up in the hall, inviting the head-warder to partake of the repasts that they brought him in their tin-dixies. The head-warder's heart was perhaps touched by the solicitude of the convicts on his behalf: for he was getting over twenty dinners offered him every day – and for nothing. But if he appreciated this thoughtfulness on the part of the convicts, he certainly did not manifest his gratitude openly. Instead, some of the things he said to those convicts, every day, reached depths of obscenity that were remarkable even for a discipline head-warder.

The next thing that happened, therefore, was that there was a strike. The convicts marched out into the yard, one day after lunch, in accordance with long-established routine. They formed up in their various spans, and were checked out by the chief warder, and were ordered to advance to their respective workshops. But instead of marching out through the mortuary gate, they stood firm. Just like that. There were a few cat-calls and a lot of slogans were shouted out about the porridge not being fit for a wart-hog to eat.

The chief warder ignored these observations. "Forward," he said again. But the leading span stood fast. The chief warder was not by temperament a man given to repeating himself. So the convicts went on standing, drawn up in long lines in the afternoon sun that shed its depressing yellow on the warders' uniforms and on the drab garb of the convicts. After a while a couple of parapet guards were brought round; they were stationed on top of the wall with their rusty machine-guns trained into the yard. But nothing much happened. The convicts got tired of shouting after a while. And they got more tired of standing to attention in the afternoon sun. And the cat-calls grew feebler. And the statements to the effect that a hippopotamus couldn't drink the soup were uttered with less conviction.

That bit of a food-strike was not very successful, taken all round. Each convict felt, after a while, that by standing firm there, in the yard and not going to work in the shops, he wasn't spiting anybody. He was only making things unnecessarily uncomfortable for himself. The warders didn't mind. They were saved the trouble of accompanying the convicts into the workshops and seeing that they kept out of mischief. With all the convicts lined up in the yard, like that, it was easy to keep watch over the whole lot of them. But it was darned irksome for the convicts, this food-strike. The sun beat down on us unmercifully, and we felt that, lousy though it was to work in the stone-yard and such places, it was nevertheless streets better than standing at attention, stiffly, and in silence, with a lot of warders in position all round to time your every movement.

Consequently, when the Governor arrived in person, some hours later, and he announced (in a voice that he tried to make sound as much like a fog-horn as possible), that he would see into the rations position himself, his remarks were greeted with a fair amount of cheering. And so, when the chief warder repeated his command, but in the reverse direction – for he now bellowed, "About turn! Back to sections! Forward!" – not a convict was pleased that the strike was at last over. It seemed a very long time, that couple of hours of standing to attention with the sun shining into your neck and the sweat pouring off your belly.

And this in spite of the fact that all time, as Oscar Wilde took the trouble to point out, passes slowly when you are in prison.

Morally, this food strike was a defeat for the convicts. Every convict in prison lost face through it. But in terms of practical politics the strike was a huge success. Because, apparently through the personal intervention of the Governor, the quality of the meals served up was much better than it had been for months. It was said that the Governor was anxious to keep the facts about the convicts' dissatisfaction over the food out of the newspapers. The Governor didn't want the prison to receive unfavourable press publicity, the convicts said. They said that the Governor was afraid of the boob getting a bad name. I thought there was something rich about this, somehow : the thought of a prison Governor not wanting a prison to get a bad name. For fear that members of the general public, getting to hear these unfavourable reports about the place, would decide not to patronise the prison, likely. And without the prison's regular six hundred customers (in the form of convicts doing six months and over) there wouldn't be a job for the warders and the head-warders and the trades-warders and the chief warder – and the Governor himself. That, at least, was what the convicts said.

Anyway, the food improved. And everybody was satisfied, except Blue-coat Verdamp. Because, as the days went by, his supporters dwindled. Even new first-offenders, who had arrived in the prison after the demonstrations were over, would know that some very important convict, whom they had not even met, had recently organised a protest demonstration that had resulted in the convicts being nowadays dished up with good food. There was no question of Alec the Ponce's headship. Even fellow-convicts who had been on bad terms with him for years, because he had stolen tobacco off them, or because he had had a stoppie dagga and had smoked it on his own, or for no other reason than that he was just a mongrel-bastard in any case – these convicts now began to show Alec the Ponce various small favours, like hauling out a tinder-box quickly to light his cigarette for him, or ostentatiously removing his red-spotted handkerchief from his jacket-pocket on a Saturday, and washing it for him, or saying, "Hallo, Alec", and offering to help him with his wheelbarrow when he was pushing it fully-loaded in the direction of the slag-heap.

You couldn't help noticing where Alec the Ponce stood with the boys, in those early days after the food disturbances had led to the convicts being served with better fare. You couldn't help noticing the tone of deference with which he was addressed. Everybody, too, now called him Alec; just plain Alec, without the addition of that approbrious descriptive epithet. (For the word "ponce", in prison argot, means "pimp", "producer", "brothel-keeper", "whore-monger".) On one occasion, even, a trades-warder in the boot-shop, in giving him a job, called him by his name, Alec, instead of by his number. You could see, from that, that even warders were anxious to get into his good books. Alec the Ponce had become a head all right: even though he was only doing four and a half years. He had blossomed out into a real old-time bigshot. He was a prison-head *par excellence* and no argument.

This was gall to Blue-coat Verdamp. He wasn't used to playing second-fiddle to a ponce, he said: to a man who would take a whore's money off her – the money she had earned until half-past three in the morning, mind you – and then sleep with her.

Blue-coat Verdamp circulated some appalling stories about Alec the Ponce's past. About some woman with both syphilis and consumption who was so far advanced in disease as not to be able to walk the streets any more; and then Alec would send her about the streets in a ricksha, to pick up men, the ricksha-boy transporting both the prostitute and her client to the door of her room – when Alec would arrive from around the corner to help lift the woman into the bed. And when this sick woman didn't earn enough, Alec the Ponce would thrash her with a piece of boot-sole nailed on to a length of plank.

Blue-coat Verdamp told all sorts of stories like that about his rival. All with the intention of discrediting him with the boys, of course. He also said that when Alec the Ponce got lashes, afterwards, for pimping, he howled so loud, with the cat-o'nine-tails curving about his spine, that members of the public, walking past the prison at that hour, on their way to work, started running at the noise. Because Alec the Ponce's yells were so shrill and piercing that these people thought it was their train. And so they started running, thinking they were late for work. That was what Blue-coat Verdamp said. But his campaign of defamation came to nothing. Alec the Ponce was securely established as the prison-head. And, if anything, these libellous stories Blue-coat Verdamp spread about him served but to enhance his prestige.

And so Blue-coat Verdamp started getting desperate. Day by day he watched the food. He was going to make a complaint. Everybody knew it. And it was going to be a sensational kind of protest. That much we could all sense. Just let the food drop ever so slightly in quality, and at one stroke Blue-coat Verdamp was going to re-establish himself as the man every convict in the prison – and every warder, too, of course – was going to look up to. If the soup or the skilly or the bread or the porridge got bad again, just once, then Blue-coat Verdamp was going to express his dissatisfaction in a way that would make Alec the Ponce look like a first-offenders' section lavatory-cleaner. Just you wait.

That was what everybody in the prison was saying. And a queer atmosphere of tension began to hang over the lunch-periods. We would come in from work, day after day, and taste our carrot-soup. No, it was quite all right. Carrot-soup was, after all only carrot-soup. And you couldn't squeal about it, as long as you could eat it. Carrot-soup was down on the diet-scale, and nothing could alter it. But then it had to taste like carrot-soup, and not like something else with which the convicts compared it. Then, one day, just when we had begun giving up hope of anything in the way of fire-works, the soup was noticeably off. No jokes. It was bad soup. Almost as bad as before the trouble started.

There is no describing that feeling of quivering ecstasy, of an almost masochistic sense of delight and fear and expectancy that took hold of the emotions of six hundred convicts that lunch-time, when they dipped their wooden spoons in their dixies and put their mouths to the soup . . . The warders were keyed up to almost the same pitch of excitement . . . Like a pale ghost that knowledge swept through the whole prison . . . The soup was crook. It was onkus. A yellow-bellied platypus couldn't drink it . . . And, yes, Blue-coat Verdamp had asked permission of his section-warder to proceed to the hall. That permission had been granted . . . The warders in their excitement forgot to lock the cells, which they were supposed to do after the last dixie of carrot-soup had been served . . . As many convicts and warders as could crowd on to the landings at the ends of the sections peered through the bars and wire-netting into the hall. In the penal section the crush was so great that the warders had to drive the convicts back with their batons . . . These warders wanted the best points of vantage for themselves . . .

Blue-coat Verdamp walked straight up to the head-warder, who was standing in front of his desk, trying to look nonchalant. But all the time he was eyeing Blue-coat Verdamp warily, out of the corner of his eye. If any man in that prison at that moment knew that there was trouble coming, that man was the head-warder in the hall. Carrying his dixie in front of him, and holding on to it with both hands, as though it was something very precious, Verdamp marched with a slow, almost trance-like gait, as though he had been smoking a large quantity of dagga. His face was very white. He approached the head-warder.

"Look what I have to put up with, sir," Blue-coat Verdamp announced.

"Food bad again, is it?" the head-warder queried, blandly. "Now, do you know what, if you give me a spoonful, I don't mind if I do taste some of it. Now, only a spoonful, mind."

That got Blue-coat Verdamp guessing, all right. It was a mighty clever move on the part of the head-warder. For the first time in the history of the prison, it would mean that when a convict had come into the hall complaining about the food, the head-warder had tasted it. Yes, it was very good strategy on the part of the head-warder. But it was also his trump card. Blue-coat Verdamp paused irresolute. He had made history in the prison. The head-warder in the hall had offered to taste his carrot-soup. That would put Blue-coat Verdamp clear above Alec the Ponce as the chief convict-head in the place. Let the head-warder drink a mouthful of that soup, in full view of all the convicts and warders looking on from the section-landings and Blue-coat Verdamp would emerge from the encounter as the hero of every convict in that prison, now and for many years to come.

The tension in the prison soared with each second that passed. Verdamp was quite close to the head-warder, now. He held out his dixie with one hand. With the other he extended his wooden spoon. The head-warder reached forward to take it.

"Drink a mouthful of that sewer-water and drop dead!" a convict roared from a landing across the way. The head-warder turned round to face the convict who had shouted that remark. The head-warder was at ease, now. He would deal with that convict. The whole thing was going to pass off without any irregularities taking place. It wouldn't be hard, to find that convict who had shouted. The section-warder would be able to help him in the search. The interruption had been most providential. He would make full use of that diversion.

And the moment the head-warder turned round – well, nobody could say very clearly, afterwards, how it all happened. It was so quick. And there was such confusion, with the spoon going one way, and the dixie of carrot soup going another way, and discipline-warders coming rushing in to the head-warder's assistance through four different grille-gates . . . Nobody could say exactly what had happened. But of the central feature of the event that occurred, the moment the head-warder's back was turned, there could be no doubt at all. And it was something that would be remembered for as long as there was a prison anywhere in the country. It was a story that would be passed on from one generation of warders and convicts to another. It was a legend that would grow only more gaudily-coloured with the centuries.

For, with the historical remark, "This is where I takes a snout on you screws," Blue-coat Verdamp had let go a flying kick at the head-warder, the moment his back was turned, and had landed his convict-boot square and solid up the head-warder's backside.

That's all there is to tell about it, of course. I can't hope to describe the pandemonium and the hullabaloo that followed, in the course of which Blue-coat Verdamp was knocked down and dragged out by half-a-dozen warders — whose numbers had increased to over a dozen by the time they had put him in irons and had locked him up in a solitary cell. Afterwards, when he was chucked into hospital, to have stitches put in his face and to have the more badly-crushed ribs on his right side removed, it was found that there was no need to have put Blue-coat Verdamp in leg-irons, because as the result of the doing he got on the way to the solitary cell he would never again, for the rest of his life, be able to walk without a crutch. But Blue-coat Verdamp had triumphed. He had made prison history. It was the first and the only time known to anybody at all who knew the inside life of prisons, that a convict had gone up to a warder — and a head-warder, on top of it — and had booted him up his behind. You can hit a warder with a pick-handle, to try and escape. You can even take a pot at a warder with a gun, if you can get hold of a gun, in order to try and make a break out of the boob. But to shoot a warder around with your boot, just to show your contempt for him — well, that was a different thing altogether. It was undreamt of. That you could try and overpower a warder and make a getaway: that was something everybody could understand and accept. And you'd get a couple of years for it. All right; and there would be no hard feelings. But what Blue-coat Verdamp had done, there in the hall, in the presence of the whole

86

prison, letting a head-warder have it with his boot up his jack, just to show him how much he despised him – well, that was something utterly and for ever without precedent.

After Verdamp came out of hospital the head-warder made a case about it, of course, and the case was too serious for the Governor to try himself; so the matter had to come before a magistrate: whereby the whole story got into the newspapers, of course – the story that a convict had kicked a prison-warder because the food was bad. And Blue-coat Verdamp got two years' imprisonment with hard labour, which he would have to serve after he had completed his current sentence: and when that would be, God alone knew. And he had to be kept in irons for six months, and also in solitary on spare diet for six months – three days in, one day out. And the magistrate also granted him authority to have a crutch made in the carpenters' shop, to help him walk back to the section each time he came out of the solitary cell. And so everything was settled very nicely.

And for at least six months, what with all that publicity, the food in the prison was really good. We lived like kings. And if there was still slime floating on top of the carrot-soup, every now and again, at all events it wasn't the kind of slime that made you feel all nauseated. And the irony of the whole situation, I often thought, during those months that followed in which the food was good, the irony of it was the fact that the man through whose energetic action this considerable improvement had been brought about, could enjoy these new and palatable meals on only rare occasions: On only one day out of every four, in fact. Because during those other three days out of each four, and for a period of six months, in terms of his sentence, he was locked up in solitary confinement on spare diet – which in those days consisted of a pint or so of rice water.

And by the time Verdamp's solitary was up, i.e., at the expiration of six months, the prison food was, of course, back to its natural, putrid level.

But before the decline became noticeable, something rather funny happened. Because of the story having got into the newspapers of the convicts' dissatisfaction with their rations, and particularly because of the unusual form in which one convict had manifested this general dissatisfaction, Head Office took cognisance of the matter. Accordingly an inspector of prisons was sent down to find out what sort of rations were in actual fact being served to the convicts. And the authorities were, as a matter of course, informed of his impending arrival. (I mean the prison authorities, including both those on the paid staff and those doing time.) There was a great deal of talk, in advance, about the fact that an inspector was coming down, on a certain day, to see for himself what the day's rations were like.

The inspector of prisons arrived. The prison kitchen rose to the occasion splendidly. We didn't get just carrot-soup, that day, but roast and two veg. And done to a turn. There was good, rich, thick gravy. You would have been lucky to get food as tasty as that in even the best class of hotel. The convicts lunched so sumptuously that next morning a large number reported sick: their starved digestive organs were unequal to the task of suddenly coping with a good meal.

That was the day the inspector of prisons paid his visit – well-advertised in advance – to enquire into the convicts' grievances about the way they were being fed.

A large number of convicts felt sore about the whole thing.

"The inspector will go back and say we're eating better than the Prime Minister," they said, "and we'll get the name for being a mob of bleaters." And so on. But most of us didn't care a damn about any consideration other than the fact that we were sitting down to a feast such as had not been spread before us in years.

Then, to the amazement of the whole prison – for the news spread very rapidly through the prison, although only a few convicts witnessed the actual incident – it was learnt that two short-time convicts had gone down into the hall, at lunch-time with the dixies containing their roast and two veg., and that they had demanded to be confronted with the inspector of prisons, and that they had said, "Even a pole-cat can't eat muck like this, sir. Will you please taste a mouthful and see?"

And the inspector of prisons had sampled their food, and he had turned purple with rage, and he had said, "God damn it! I don't get food like this every day. So this is the kind of food you complain about! I've never encountered such audacity in my life."

How was the inspector to guess that the head-warder in the

hall, through the promise of getting them cushy jobs in the clothing store, had got those two short-time convicts to go up and make that complaint? For days afterwards the head-warder was observed to be wearing a fat sort of a smile on his face.

Excursion

During the fourth year of my imprisonment, a very beautiful thing happened to me. I was working in the carpenters' shop still. A bracket had to be fitted into a guard-post on the pavement in front of the prison. The head-warder sent me out to do this job. I went there, escorted by a discipline-warder and accompanied by another convict. It was a wonderful adventure. Even now, when I think of it, twenty years later, that old thrill comes back to me once more.

"Get your tools," the head-warder said to me, "And the timber for a bracket." To the discipline-warder he said, "Get your gun."

So we went out through the back-gate of the prison, the warder, the other convict and I. At the gate the warder got his revolver which he slung over his shoulder on a strap. The other convict and I were searched. The outside-warder opened the gate. Slowly, much too slowly, the gate creaked outward on its heavy iron hinges – and we saw the outside world.

Stout Cortez seeing the Pacific for the first time, from a peak on Darien . . . All that sentimental rubbish. As though one piece of ocean could be different from any other piece of ocean . . .

But in that moment of the gate swinging open very slowly, I saw the outside world again, after a period of four years.

"Forward," the discipline-warder said.

It sounded like the voice of Divinity talking. It meant we were going down that road which I had seen only once before, four years ago, and the sight of which had made my throat contract. because I had been under the sentence of death, then, and as we had approached the gloomy exterior of the prison, and those forbidding-looking portals had reared up before me, it was with an unutterable despair that I had looked on that same road. for the last time.

We continued down that road, towards the front of the prison, where the guard-post was. Several times the discipline-warder had to shout at me to pick up my step. For every moment was ecstasy to me. I walked with an awful deliberation. I wanted to miss nothing. I wanted to go as slow as possible; those moments that we were outside the prison had to stretch as long as days and hours and years; oh, we hadn't to go at more than a snail's pace. And I saw to it that we didn't. The warder could shout his head off. This dreadful ecstasy had to linger.

I have never in my life, before or since, beheld a scene as entrancing in its splendour as what I viewed from that dusty road, that was impregnated with a heady fragrance – that dusty red road skirting the prison. I have seen Funchal from the sea; I have walked those cobbled roads, green with young grass-blades like sprinkled confetti, and I couldn't see what there was in Madeira to thrill the tourists, who all said, "Oh," and "Oh," as though it was paradise. And I have seen middle-aged men standing in St. James' park and looking over the bridge at the part of London on the other side of Whitehall, with the early light of a summer morning on it : and I wondered what they saw in it. And the Paris boulevards, and in Brussels, the Avenue Louise, and all sorts of other places and scenes – and among them, not least, the Hex River mountains from the train-window. I have seen lots of sights – since that day when I walked out of the back-gate of the prison, to go and put up that bracket at the guard-post. And all those sights have left me cold.

I don't think that even love has had for me the warmth and the beauty and the deep-drawn delight that came to me on that road, red with perfumed dust, skirting the prison. Love. Well, I was young. And I was in love with the whole world. And life had not yet been made sick for me through the poison of introspection. And so I walked slowly in spite of the discipline-warder's bellowings, in order to miss nothing, in order that this incredible joy that had come to me suddenly and undeservedly, should fill my entire being, dropping rose-petals on the places where my shoulders were bruised.

It was a dream-world that I walked into. For four years I had been dreaming of a moment such as this was. I was outside. It was all *world*. I was walking along a road where free people walked – men and women and children : and, above all, women. Sunlight and shadow and distance played queer tricks with my eyes. Because I had been confined within cramped walls for four years, my eyes were unable to accommodate themselves to the majesty of distance. To be able to see far away – fruit-trees a long way off, for instance, and a white-washed fence at the bottom of the road: all these things were very beautiful. They were invested with the magic of strangeness. I was in a painted world, queerly different from what I had expected the outside to be. I had so forgotten common things, that when I saw a couple of fowls in a back-yard I stopped and stared at them in an unspeakable joy.

For four years I had only memories of what the world was really like. And what I saw now, distance and hues, and pale lights and patches of grass: they no longer corresponded with my ideas about them. They were quite different from my memories of them. And they were even more lovely than I had expected them to be.

For years I had dreamt of the world. I had tried, in the nights when I had lain awake, to recall that gaudy lost world that I had known up to the time when I was twenty. And I saw now that it was less brightly-coloured than I had pictured it to be. But I was not disappointed. On the contrary, this pallid reality was something infinitely more exquisite than my black and scarlet visionings of it had been.

We got to the guard-post much too soon. But before we entered it a woman and a girl came past: the wife and daugher of a warder. And they didn't look at us of course. Because this was on the prison reserve, where they lived; and so they were used to seeing convicts.

But I stared at them, at this woman and girl. I couldn't look at them enough, I had to see them, and I had to remember. I had to remember everything about them, every detail of how they looked, and what they felt like. I had to remember everything about what that divine moment of their nearness did to my senses, and every single detail of their faces and their bodies and their eyes and their dresses, and the folds in their frocks, and the crinkles in the woman's legs, at the back of her knees, and the way their bodies swayed when they walked, and the way their light, summery dresses fluttered in the breeze when they walked. Above all, I had to remember that sublime impact on my soul, on my blood, of their having passed close to me. I must not forget that feeling of thick silence that was fragrant with the inside of them.

For I had to remember all that when I was locked up again. I had to treasure it all up; not a drop of it was to be spilt; and I did, as a matter of fact, succeed in keeping that memory vivid for at least a year after that – perhaps even longer.

That woman's dress was short. I hadn't expected that. How was I to know that women's fashions had undergone so much change during the four years in which I was shut away from the sound and the sight of all women? And the little girl's frock was a washed-out sort of blue. I don't mean that the colour really was washed out of course, it was only that I had expected the colours of materials to be more startling-hued than what they actually were. And I knew, instantly, that those really were the colours of the outside world, the colours of trees and the colours of dresses. I knew immediately that that girl wasn't wearing a faded dress. It was only that I had, during the years, come to imagine, in waking dreams of the outside world, that there was a brilliance about those things of living and the acts of living which was not really there.

But, of course, this pallor only enhanced the incredible miracle of the life that people live. It made the mystery all the more refined. The glitter was all the more alluring because it was subdued. Life was washed out, faded. So its attractiveness was a haunted thing. The outside world was deadly artistry.

After the bracket had been nailed into place, the convict who went with me having made holes in the wall with the cold chisel in the places where I showed him – mine being the higher-up job of hammering in the plugs and securing the bracket – we went back along the road we had come. But this time the convict who had come with me joined with the warder in making us hurry up. For it was getting on towards lunch-time, and my convict-colleague was hungry. He was only a short-timer; so in the walk between the guard-post and the back-gate of the prison there was little novelty for him.

But this time I didn't mind hurrying. I had already seen so much. I had a whole world of things to remember in the days to come. I had been allowed into fairy-land. I had thrilled to the earth and its beauty and its secrets. The faces and the figures of that woman and girl had not come up to my expectations in respect of the dark loveliness that I had come to associate with woman. But their beauty seemed all the more ethereal because it was not held fast in swift contours and vivid colouring. And their beauty had become all the more intangible because it had made contact with my senses not as spirit but as clay. Paradise was so much nearer to me than the soil, during those years of my dreaming of the outside world. And what there was of clay in that girl and woman was a thing of far greater mystery to me than their quality of soul.

Reality was more trancelike than a vision, more breath-taking than any dream.

During the many months that followed, of my sojourning inside the walls, that saunter along the dusty road was a warm and luscious memory for me. It was an excursion into realms of gaudy adventure where my sight had been dazzled with shining fresh flowers and my ears had been filled with the sound ot old gold. And life had been broken open like a ripe pomegranate, and tropical fronds had bent low in laughter, and spring had exulted in the stillness of young growth.

I had tiptoed down the corridors of ancient palaces, richly arrassed and niched with armorial bearings; my footsteps had wandered through sacred groves. And I would look at my feet, alone in my cell for many nights thereafter; and I would think that these feet, shod in these same boots, had walked down that road, once, and had got red dust on them, had walked in the same dust in which people of the outside world had walked, in which that girl and that woman had walked. And thinking like that I would not feel cut off from the world at all. For my boots were tangible proof that I was one with the earth and with life; proof – that any court of law would accept – that I belonged with people.

And, of course, the immediate effect of my adventure in Avalon was that my dreamings of the outside world became again exotic things of black and scarlet, heavy with perfumes, low-hung with the night. In my visionings the world outside the prison was invested with more vivid colours than ever before . . .

(Only the other day I passed that same spot again, by car. After an interval of twenty years. And the red road had been tarred. And I saw then that the whole distance we had walked, the distance from the back-gate to the guard-post, which still stood there on the corner – with the bracket still in place, no doubt, for I had nailed it in solid – was less than a hundred yards.)

Madness

I was back in the section, back to the cells and the workshops and the daily grind. The going was rather terrible. With my sanity in the balance, as I knew it to be, I went through hell. I am not going to try to explain what I suffered. Every moment, almost, I thought I would go right off my rocker and start raving. At other times I was obsessed with the fear of a warder or a fellow-convict spotting the madness in my eyes, and giving me a wide berth, in consequence: and I knew that whoever spotted my insanity would pass on that information to somebody else, and so on. And then, no matter how hard I played sane, I would be classed as a lunatic. And every time, at night, when the steel door was banged shut on me by the warder, and I heard the key grate in the lock, then my head would start spinning, and I would crawl round and round on the concrete floor of my cage, round and round, with great difficulty, on my hands and knees, because of the narrowness of the walls of the cage. I would crawl round and round, like that, until I would drop down from exhaustion. And yet I had a strange cunning, with all this. I would time myself. The warders, coming along the corridor at hourly intervals and looking in through one peep-hole after another, would never catch me out crawling round and round the steel cage. Whenever I sensed that the warder was almost due I would grab up a book, any sort of a book, and I would sit down on the floor and pretend to read. And as soon as I had seen the warder's eye appear at the peep-hole I would resume my crawling. On hands and knees, round and round. I got very good at this crawling, after a while. I crawled very noiselessly. And I had got the trick of pulling in my buttocks, in just the right way, at each corner, so that I just rubbed my backside against the steel partitionings each time I made a full turn.

One night the warder came back again, unexpectedly, after he had looked in once and had seen me sitting on the floor, pretending to read.

And so he caught me crawling, like that. And for a couple of moments after he had shouted out and asked me what I was doing, I was terrified. I thought he had collared me dead to rights, now, and the whole thing would come out and it would be me booked for the bughouse.

But I didn't lose my head. And I answered quickly.

"I am looking for my ticket-pocket, sir," I replied, getting up from the floor and going to talk to the warder through the peephole.

"But what you want your bleeding ticket-pocket for this time of the night?" the warder demanded.

"The ticket-pocket came off my jacket, sir," I explained, "and so I started looking for it."

"That's a funny thing to do," the warder said, and he sounded nonplussed, "crawling around on your hands and knees like you're mad, looking for your ticket-pocket."

"It wasn't the ticket-pocket I wanted, actually," I said to the warder. "What I actually was after was the ticket inside the ticket-pocket. I wanted to work out how much time I still got to do."

My brain was working very fast. I felt I could outwit a dozen warders, and also the whole world. Lord, they'd never tumble to it that I was mad! I had all sorts of illusions of grandeur, suddenly. Let them come! I could do the most ridiculous things, and I could get away with it. I had a brain that could think out the most plausible excuses for the blackest kind of insanity that came out of my mad guts.

The warder looked at the card on my cage door. He read out my name, crime, sentence, date of conviction, date of discharge, prison number, religion and workshop.

"Well, you still got quite a few years to do," he announced, after having, apparently, done a bit of mental arithmetic.

"Yes, sir," I answered, "but I wanted to calculate it exactly. You see, I get a quarter off, for first offender's good conduct remission, and six months special mitigation for the Flag Bill (we all got that off, you know, sir), and two months off because of the Prince of Wales' visit, and another . . ."

"You bastards get far too much time off," the warder interrupted me curtly. "The authorities must be mad to give you time off like that."

He had said that the authorities were mad. That gave me more confidence than ever. I didn't feel so lonely and cut off from the rest of mankind, in my insanity. Here were the authorities also mad. I had the warder's word for it. I had a sudden, vivid picture of the authorities also crawling round and round on the floors of their bedrooms. It cheered me up no end, that ridiculous thought of the authorities also having to be careful of the way they manipulated their buttocks round the corners . . .

Release

Those last eight months passed quickly. As a matter of fact, it turned out that it was a bit more than eight months. The clerk at head office in charge of my files had omitted to make certain calculations in respect of remission, with the result that, for some time, I was in the queer position of being a forgotten man. I have difficulty, even to-day, in explaining what that means. The day I was due for discharge I said to my section-warder, in the morning, "I am going out to-day," and I added, "I suppose I stay in the section until they send for the discharges, sir?"

The section-officer said, no, he hadn't been notified. But he knew I was going out, of course, quite soon. I had it on my ticket. And he knew that I had been measured for a suit. Anyway, I showed the section-warder my ticket, and we got a pencil and a piece of paper and we worked it out together. There was no doubt about it. I was due for discharge, and right away.

"Anyway, I got no instructions," the section-warder said. "Fall in for work."

And in the workshop I showed my ticket to the head-warder, and he also worked out the figures, and he scratched his head, and looked puzzled. "But I can't do nothing about it," he assured me. "That's for the discipline staff. I am only a trades head-warder. So get on with your blooming job."

And I showed my ticket to a whole lot of convicts, and they worked it out, also, not with paper and pencil, because they didn't need to. A convict who had done lots of stretches only had to take a single glance at my ticket and through some sort of sixth sense, because he had done so much time, he could see at once that I was due for discharge.

"They must a lorst your papers at head-office," one blue-coat suggested. "That means you'll never get out. You don't exist for them no more. I remember the case of . . ."

98

But I moved away quickly. I didn't want to hear any bad-luck stories. I was scared of ill-omened precedents.

Next day I saw the chief warder in the office about my getting discharged. He also agreed with me that as far as the law was concerned I was a free man. It said so on my ticket.

"Yes," I acknowledged, "I am free. I am a free man. There's nothing to keep me here in prison any more. Nothing except the bars and the locks and the warders."

Anyway, the chief warder informed me that it was no concern of his. All these things were done from head-office. All he could do was, when a discharge-warrant came from head-office for a convict, to order that convict's release. And he hadn't got such a discharge warrant from head-office for me. "But don't you worry," he assured me. "The moment that paper comes along, I'll see you get out. I won't keep you here a minute longer than I got to."

I thanked him very much. But was there nothing he could do about it?

"It seems to me like the clerk in charge of your file has sort of overlooked it," the chief warder said. "Or he may be on leave. Or he may have forgotten to enter some of your remission – over the Flag Bill, perhaps. Or he may have lost your papers. I remember a case . . ."

But I asked the chief warder please not to continue. I was afraid I might panic. If nothing was heard during the course of the next few days, might he perhaps take it up with the head-office? He assured me that he would. "If you don't hear any more about it," he said, "Come and see me again in about a month's time."

I went to see him again, of course. And in much less than a month's time.

"But see, sir," I said, "I am here, am I not? And according to the details of my sentence and remission I have no right to be here. In theory I am not a hard-labour convict at all."

"What do you want, then?" the chief warder enquired, in a nasty tone. "Do you want a job here as chief warder, perhaps? Don't be afraid to ask, now."

But I informed him, trying hard to keep sane, that I didn't want any sort of job in the prison, and that my one desire was to get as far away as possible from any contact with and any thought of the prison.

"It's your file at head-office," the chief warder explained. "Yes, something must have happened about your file. I'll go and see about it next chance I get of slipping away from the prison for an hour or so."

"Might that be to-day, sir, perhaps?" I enquired hopefully.

"Some time next month," the chief warder answered. "Look, you've done a good long stretch, already, and we haven't had much trouble from you. I hope you aren't going to start being a nuisance now. What's a few extra months, anyway, on top of the time you have already done with a clean sheet? Just go back to the section, and enjoy yourself here a little longer, and it will all get fixed up."

I passed through a period of the most utter desolation. I felt so completely helpless and frustrated. And there was nothing I could do about it. I still get nightmares about that period. Here was I, in the prison, a human being, of flesh and air and bone; I existed here, in the prison, as a physical reality. At least, that was what I had always believed. But I found that I wasn't that person at all. I wasn't me. I wasn't this individual sitting here on a stool eating mealie-porridge out of a tin basin. Oh, no. This person did not exist at all, as an entity. It wasn't me, that had got his suit made— the suit that was all pressed and hung on a clothes-hanger in the tailors' shop, waiting for me to come and fetch it away. No, I wasn't this person at all.

What was really me was a lot of papers, dog-eared and yellowed with the years, lying between two cardboard covers and tied up with green string, in a filing cabinet at head-office . . . I saw, now, why I had got claustrophobia, in prison. It wasn't because of the prison. Quite enough air came into my cage through the barred window. But that person in the steel cage wasn't me at all. My real individuality, my real me, were those papers in that filing-cabinet. So, of course, I had suffocation fears. Who wouldn't get claustrophobia, shut like that between two covers, and tied up with green string, and then locked away into a steel cabinet—with more and more folders getting piled on top of me with each year that passed? How on earth can you breathe inside a steel cabinet?

But I don't want to go on piling up the horrors. It is enough to say that, shortly afterwards, through the friendly offices of the chief warder, a vast stack of other folders were lifted from me, and

I was taken out of the steel cabinet, and my covers were dusted, and the green string was untied . . .

As a result of this bit of confusion, I didn't get discharged from the prison, like other convicts, at nine o'clock in the morning. The warrant for my release arrived late one afternoon. It was marked urgent, in very large, black letters and it said that I was to be released immediately.

So they had to fetch a clerk from his home (because he had already gone off duty) to work out how much was due to me in gratuity and to make out an official cheque for me. Another warder escorted me to the stores, where they fitted me out with a pair of prison-made discharge boots. They went and dug up my suit-case, containing a couple of shirts that I had worn many years ago, before I was convicted. I put on a shirt with stripes. The cool, luxurious feel of light linen against my skin after all those years in which I had worn the coarse, stinking, degrading – oh, never mind: the sensation of linen lying lightly on my body was exquisite. There was also a tie in my suit-case, a bright piece of neckwear that had not faded, very appreciably, during the length of time in which it had been thrust away from the world, in a dark corner. They had not put me in prison, alone, but my few poor possessions also. I didn't realise, until now, that I had had my suitcase and my socks and my shirts to keep me company during the period of my incarceration. I picked up that tie with a warm feeling of intimacy. My friendly old tie; my companion in imprisonment; here we were meeting again; and he was still gaudy; he still had memories of former gaieties, brightly-dyed; he was still half-cheeky. I wondered whether I was like my tie in this respect; whether I also, at the end of my imprisonment, retained something inside me that was bright-hued. But I feared not. My tie didn't have to say "Yes, sir," all day long.

And then, of course, when I had it round my neck, I didn't know how to fasten that tie. Through all that long disuse my fingers had lost the trick of knotting a tie around my neck. A warder performed the office for me.

And then I found that I couldn't get my suit. It was locked up in the tailor's shop. They couldn't get the key. It was a blow. But they fitted me out with an ordinary prison discharge suit, called a pom-pom, which the Government supplies to short-timer discharged convicts. It didn't look very elegant, but they said it would do for the night. Next morning I could call round at the prison, at the front-gate, and my blue serge suit would be neatly parcelled-up there for me.

"Please see to it that they don't crush my suit when they fold it," I said to a discipline-warder. But I hadn't much faith that they would exercise the right amount of care.

The final formalities were gone through. I was given my discharge papers. It was explained to me that mine was a conditional release. I was being let out on ticket-of-leave. The conditions of my discharge were read out to me: they were contained in two pages of print. Then I shook hands with the warders about me and I took up my suit-case and my prison-discharge boots sounded clumsy on the cement-floor of the court-yard before the main gate. And the gate swung open. Not very much. Just enough to let me out.

And I was free.

The guard at the gate shook hands with me. And he called me by my name instead of by my number.

"Look after yourself, now," the gate-warder said. "You know boob is a bastard. See you don't come back."

I answered, "Yes, thank you, sir."

Forgetting that I no longer had any need to call him "sir".

FROM *A Cask of Jerepigo* (1957)

A posthumous selection of sketches published in *South African Opinion* and *Trek* between 1944 and 1950.

Street Processions

For as long as I can remember, almost, street processions have been in my blood. When I see a long line of people marching through the streets – the longer the line, the better I like it – something primordial gets stirred inside me and I am overtaken by the urge to fall in also, and take my place somewhere near the end of the procession. I have no doubt that the reason why, many years ago – before Communism had the social standing and prestige which it enjoys to-day – the reason why in my youth I joined the Young Communist League in Johannesburg was because that part of Socialist ideology which consisted of organising processions through the streets, holding up the traffic and all that sort of thing, made a very profound appeal to my ethical sense.

And it has been like that with me all my life.

There is something about the sight and the thought of a long line of men marching through the streets of a city that fills me with an awe that I can't define very easily. And it has got to be through a city. A procession through a village or just over the veld isn't the same thing. And the people taking part in it should be mostly men. One or two women are all right, too, perhaps. But there shouldn't be too many of them. Banners are optional. And while I am not too keen on a band, I can overlook its presence.

The ideal conditions for a procession are grey skies and wet streets. And there should be a drizzle. My tastes don't run to the extremes of a blizzard or a tropical downpour. Thunder and lightning effects are out of place. All you want is a steady drip-drip of fine rain that makes everything look bleak and dismal, without the comfortable abandonment of utter desolation. Then through these drab streets there must come trailing a long line of humanity, walking three or four abreast, their boots muddy and their clothes (by preference) shabby and shapeless in the rain, and their faces a grey pallor. They can sing a little, too, if they like, to try and cheer themselves up – without ever succeeding, of course. And in this sombre trudging – the dull tramp awakening no echoes – of thousands of booted feet on cobbles or tarred road, there goes my heart, also. I get gripped with an intense feeling of being one with stupid, struggling, rotten, heroic humanity, and in this grey march there is a heavy symbolism whose elements I don't try to interpret for fear that the parts should together be less than the whole; and I find myself, contrary to all the promptings of good sense and reason, yielding to the urge to try and find a place for myself somewhere near the tail end of the procession.

Oh, and of course, there is another thing, something I had almost forgotten, and that is the *cause* operating as the dynamism for getting a procession of this description organised and under way. Frankly, I don't think the cause matters very much. I have a natural predilection for an unpopular cause and, above all, for a forlorn cause – a lost hope, and whether this peculiar idiosyncrasy of mine springs from ordinary perversity, or from a nobility of soul, is something that I have not been able to ascertain. And so, while I always feel that it is very nice, and all that, if the march is undertaken by the participants in a spirit of lofty idealism, because a very important principle is at stake, I am equally satisfied, provided that the afore-stipulated conditions of muddy boots and grey skies are present, if the spiritual factors back of the demonstration are not so very high or altruistic.

This weakness of mine in the way of desiring to make one with street processions, identifying myself with and merging my personality in a mass of humanity moving onwards to no clearly defined goal, has in the past resulted in my becoming on more than one occasion involved in a considerable measure of embarrassment. In my youth, for instance, when the Salvation Army moved up from the town hall steps at the termination of a Sunday evening open-air meeting, and I found myself marching on at the back, in a sort of trance, it happened at least twice that I followed the procession right into the Hope Hall in Commissioner Street, with the result that, each time, I wasn't able to get out again until I had been converted.

And then, only a couple of years ago, with the annual Corpus

Christi procession to the End Street Convent, when I had again from force of habit taken my place near the end of the line and was proceeding down Bree Street, feeling very solemn as I always do on such occasions, I realised, suddenly, the incongruity of my presence in the company of priests in black vestments and stoles and choirboys in white surplices, and all carrying missals, while I was dressed just in civvies and half a loaf of bread under my arm, which I was taking home for supper . . . as I explained to an abbot-looking gentleman in a mitre, who hadn't said anything about my being in that procession, but who seemed unhappy, nevertheless, in a peculiar sort of a way.

Similarly, I have, at different times, marched through the streets of London with Communists, Mosleyites, Scotchmen on their way to the Cup-Tie, unemployed Welsh miners and the Peace Pledge Union.

The last time I marched in a procession was as recently as last Saturday afternoon. I was on my way home, when from the top of the Malvern tram I spotted in front of Jeppe Station a street procession in course of formation. I could see straight away that the conditions were just right. It was drizzling. The streets were wet and grey and muddy. The sky was bleak and cheerless. I prepared to alight. Unfortunately, however, the tram was very crowded, with the result that I wasn't able to get off before the Berg Street stop. From there I took another tram back to Jeppe Station, arriving there just as the procession was moving off. I took my place somewhere near the rear. We marched in a northerly direction and swung into Commissioner Street. Trudge. Trudge. Drizzle. Mud. Wet boots and shapeless clothes. I didn't ask what the procession was about. I didn't want to reveal my ignorance and chance getting sneered at. I had been sneered at by a procession before to-day, and I don't like it.

"It's that (so-and-so) Steyn," the man on the left of me remarked by way of conversation.

"You're telling me," I answered.

He *was* telling me, of course. Otherwise I wouldn't know what it was all about.

"If it wasn't for him," the man on my left continued, "Us miners wouldn't be on strike."

"Us miners wouldn't be," I agreed, relieved to have discovered, so soon, what the procession was all about.

A middle-aged man in front of me, in a khaki overcoat, was singing rather a lot. A young fellow with a free and easy sort of look marched next to him. On my right was a stocky man with a grey moustache and a red rosette.

"You know," this stocky, grey-moustached man remarked to me after a while, "in 1922 it was different. In 1922 I was shooting yous. In 1922 I was in the police. Now I am one of yous."

The imp of perversity inside me egged me on to pick a quarrel with Grey-Moustache.

"How do I know that you still aren't one of thems?" I enquired.

Grey-Moustache's neck went all red.

"I am a rock-buster on the Crown Mines," he retorted. "There's half-a-dozen men in this procession as knows I am a rock-buster on the Crown Mines."

In this way what had at first promised to be an unpleasant incident was settled peaceably. Only, I couldn't help feeling that in the depth of his most secret sincerities Grey-Moustache was still one of thems. As the old saying goes, if you're once one of thems, you're always one of thems.

So the march continued in the grey drizzle. Wet clothes and boots and mud-splashed trouser-tops. A number of low songs were sung. Various obscene remarks were made. Everything was in order.

A big fat man in a black overcoat was acting as a sort of linesman for our part of the procession. They called him Oom Tobie. He was a kind of cheer-leader. He would hurry on until he got about fifty yards ahead of our rank, and then he would stand on the pavement and shout out the slogans. These were in the form of questions to which the procession roared out the answers. As far as I could make out, it all had a lot to do with the miners' democratic rights.

"Do we want Steyn?" Oom Tobie would ask.

"No!" the procession would roar. That seemed to be the right answer.

"Do we want the capitalists?" Oom Tobie would ask again.

"No!" would come the thunderous reply.

Then Oom Tobie would look sort of arch, like a school-teacher trying to tip his class off as to the right thing to answer, with the inspector present, and he would shout out: "But – do we want democracy?"

I make the acknowledgement – and gladly – that a considerable proportion of the miners shouted "Yes!" But it was also a fact that an equal number would answer, with the same degree of determination, "No!" It seemed to me that Oom Tobie had not properly rehearsed them in their responses. He didn't seem to have given them the proper instructions on this point. I came to the conclusion that Oom Tobie wasn't himself too sure as to what was the right answer either.

Trudge. Tramp. Grey faces. Dirty songs. Everything was going very nicely. Then, near Delvers Street, somewhere, the procession came to a halt. Oom Tobie, water dripping from his black over-coat but his face beaming, came and made a further announce-ment. "The West Rand boys is here, now," he said, "and we are going up Jeppe Street. And when you get to the 'Rand Daily Mail' building, stand there and boo your guts out."

Everybody, myself included, looked forward to booing his guts out in front of the "Rand Daily Mail" offices. But I don't know what good it did. There seemed to be only a few clerks and subs and typistes looking out of the first and second floor windows, and at the first blast of all those raspberries they drew back and went and hid somewhere. But nobody appeared in any window of the works department. Thus, after twenty years in journalism, I was denied the opportunity – which had so nearly come my way – of telling a comp what I thought of him.

It was after we had passed the "Rand Daily Mail" offices that I realised why the man in the khaki overcoat and the free-and-easy youth were singing more loudly than anybody else. By that time they were not only singing, but also staggering. They had a bottle of Jeripigo wine which they were passing backwards and forwards and from which they were taking surreptitious swigs. Grey-Moustache reported the matter to Oom Tobie. As I have remarked before, once one of thems, always one of thems. Nevertheless, I have rarely seen a man as indignant as Oom Tobie was at that moment. And I am sure that not even an underground manager had ever dressed down Khaki Overcoat and the free-and-easy youth in terms of vituperation such as Oom Tobie employed now.

"You are giving us all a bad name," he shouted finally. "Drinking wine like that out of the bottle, and in the street. And in front of the 'Rand Daily Mail,' too. What if they had taken your photograph, drinking wine, when all the boys was booing? What if they got your photo like that in the 'Rand Daily Mail' on Monday morning?"

"But we did boo, too," the free-and-easy youth explained. "In between."

"Won't you have a pull at the bottle, too, Oom Tobie?" the man in the khaki overcoat asked. "Just a small one, Oom Tobie?"

"Well, seeing it's you," Oom Tobie replied, "and because it's raining to-day – but not for any other reason, mind you – I don't mind if I just have a small mouthful. But don't let anybody see. Don't pass me the bottle until that tram has gone round the corner."

A few minutes later the procession reached the town hall steps and I made a dash for home. But as there wasn't a Malvern tram in sight, I sauntered into a pub. I asked for a Jerepigo. I found it was good stuff.

The Old Magistrate's Court

A few days ago I stood in a spacious courtyard surrounded with dun-coloured walls. The doors opening into the courtyard were few but massive; the windows were covered with rusty bars. Many years before, when I stood on that same spot and looked at those barred apertures, I thought that they were like a woman's eyes, heavily fringed with dark lashes. Now they seemed to be simply like windows with iron bars stuck in front of them.

The place where I stood was the yard of the Old Magistrates' Courts, in Johannesburg. To-day the building is no longer a court-house, but is used as offices of the Governor-General's Fund and for other purposes. But they don't seem to have found any use for the yard itself, which for half a century was the temporary place of detention for the city's awaiting trial prisoners. Europeans and natives, men and women. Whatever was the charge against them, those accused of transgressing the law were brought into the yard of the Magistrate's Court. They came on foot, handcuffed and under escort, or they were conveyed there by Black Maria.

Through the forbidding-looking portals opening on to New Street South the prisoners were conducted – quietly led, in most cases, cajoled or enticed sometimes, or occasionally simply pushed from behind – into the yard, there to remain until their cases had been disposed of. Which meant that they were either sentenced or acquitted in a summary trial by the magistrate, if the charges against them were not serious; or else they appeared on a preliminary examination, to be committed for trial at the Supreme Court.

It was warm and sunny, that afternoon of a few days ago, when I stood alone in that courtyard, at the beginning of a new spring, and I was surprised to find how little the place had changed. The walls had always seemed just so dilapidated, with the same patches of weathered plaster, yellow like old parchment, and the same extensive areas of exposed and discoloured brickwork. There seemed to be still the same cracks in the dirty grey of the cement floor : those fissures might have widened and deepened a little, with the years; but I couldn't tell. They seemed just the same, anyway.

And the blue enamel basin, fixed to a wall under a tap, was invested with that peculiar sort of squalor which becomes imparted to all inanimate things that have for long lived very closely to the raw things of human life.

The place had not changed. The walls were redolent of yesterdays that had lost their bitterness; they breathed of spectral longagos, of ancient, sullied things.

The only way in which the present differed from the past – in which this afternoon was not the same as some other, vanished, afternoon, when the same sun shone down on brick and stone and concrete – was that now the prison-yard was silent. But it was not an oppressive stillness. It was a tranquillity charged with a spirit of gentle melancholy, like when a single late violet is left growing on a bank where a little while before there were a myriad clusters.

And as in the perfume of violets, in that quiet there was a heady fragrance, maddening to the senses, so that that prison-yard seemed to come alive again, for a little while, and the fat gaoler seated in front of the heavy door, in the far corner, was not a ghost but a stony reality; and the native warders were again marshalling their charges, making them stand up or sit down in rows; and the white prisoners, if they were new to the ways of a goal, were clamouring at a little barred window about getting messages sent to their friends for bail to the cynical amusement of the police and the old offenders, who did not expect to see the outside world again for many years, if at all, and who had other, more serious concerns. And a couple of street-walkers were once more looking into the cracked piece of mirror over the blue-enamel wash-basin, putting paint on their lips and then wiping it off again, uncertain as to what would make a better impression on the magistrate who was to try them for soliciting.

For a little while, because of the silence pervading that yard which for 50 years had been a prison and was now open to any member of the public to stroll about in, there resounded once more within those walls the clank of fetters. In that dilapidated yard there was awakened again, for a few moments, that sombre activity of men and women languishing in bondage that is more stark than the dilapidation of crumbling plaster. Deserted of its tenants for ever, the yard in the Old Magistrates' Courts, for the first time since it was built, did not seem to be derelict.

I would recommend the artist or the writer, or any man or woman who is interested in that strange and brooding and carnal-twilight thing that we call "atmosphere" to pay a visit to this place. For I don't suppose it will be long, now, before they pull those old buildings down. And remember, as you walk the yard and your footsteps echo because of the silence, that there are ghosts from the past that walk beside you.

And for a few moments may the place come alive for you also.

The glint of the spring sunshine on the handcuffs. On tarnished people and on dreams that have gone. The gaudy scarf which a man will wear around his neck only a little longer: the scarf is shortly going to be replaced with a rope. The stained handwriting on the letter from his sweetheart which the forger pulls out of his pocket, surreptitiously – gloomily wondering why there is such a thing in the world as handwriting. The blue haze in which a native prisoner is puffing at a dagga-cigarette, in the lavatory, while his accomplice watches the door. The crimson lipstick on the mouth of the harlot, as vivid now as it was twenty years ago. And the *corpus delicti.* And the placid clouds in the sky overhead. And the detectives. And the pallid terrors in the hearts of men.

As for me, I found, when I eventually turned to depart, that the massive door, because it moved so heavily on its rusted hinges, refused, for a few moments, to open.

Ghosts

I read a small news item the other day about a Cape Town gentleman who complained that his life was being made difficult for him on account of ghosts. His house was haunted, he said; his children were terrified and his servants were wanting to leave; how he felt about it himself was not revealed in the newspaper report; perhaps he didn't want to say.

I wasn't surprised at this man's servants reacting in that way, especially if they were Cape Coloureds or Malays, who are almost as quick as Zulus at detecting the presence of ghosts about a place.

Is there such a thing as a ghost, anyway? Well, I do know that I have never come across a ghost or any other kind of a spirit manifestation at an orthodox spiritualist seance. In fact, to a person who is afraid of ghosts, I would have no hesitation in recommending an attendance or two at a spiritualist seance, when whatever fears he might have in regard to the things of the spirit-world would be dissipated for him, through his being brought to a sane realisation of the fact that there isn't such a thing as the spirit-world.

But outside of a spiritual research meeting-place I am not so sure about there not being ghosts.

I once saw a ghost on the Pretoria road. It was near where the road branches off to Robert's Heights. And it was round about midnight. Afterwards, when it wasn't night time any more, I was no longer certain that it was a ghost that I saw there. I began to think that it might possibly have been a native riding a push-bike across the veld and then riding it up the trunk of a blue-gum and along some of the lower branches, doing the latter part of his ride with his head hanging down. I didn't watch what he did after that, because it was a lonely part of the veld, at midnight, and I thought that what I was seeing was a ghost.

It is for this reason that superstition dies hard. People just don't pause to reflect. They simply say, straight out, "That's a ghost," whereas, in actual fact, there is always a rational explanation for any kind of (apparently) ghostly phenomenon. What I saw on the Pretoria road, and what my imagination took to be a ghost, was nothing more than a native performing acrobatics on a push-bike. Oh, and I also forgot to say that his neck was about two feet long, and curved.

But it doesn't matter very much whether or not we believe in ghosts; because, in any case, we'll have ghosts with us always. And if not real ghosts, then, at all events, real ghost stories – which are, I suppose, even better.

What great ghosts have we got from the past? What pale phantoms are wandering by the monuments of Rome and Thebes, or gliding by the blackened stones that once formed part of Ilium's topless towers, or huddled by the ruins of Babylon and Memphis? Majestic spectres haunting history's deathless places – no, I can think of none.

I can think of no great ghosts from the long ago; ghosts that grip my imagination even as much as does the cycling native performing acrobatic feats off the Pretoria road. (Oh, and there is something else I forgot: from the waist downwards he was semi-transparent).

From the Old Testament I can remember, off-hand, Saul's encounter with the ghost of the prophet Samuel. But in that frightening tale I am more impressed with the personality of the Witch of Endor than with Samuel's ghost. And with the Old Testament we are coming from the ghost to the ghost story. And it is natural, here, to make allusion to Banquo's ghost. And to the ghost in Hamlet – whose main significance for me is the fact that Shakespeare once played him. I have often wondered if the Elizabethan producers always picked out the more dud roles for Shakespeare: you know, jealousy and all that: anybody can write Hamlet, sort of thing, but it takes a real classy actor to play him.

Literature, of course – fiction – is packed full of ghosts. But fiction is different from history. At least, I suppose that is what an historian would maintain, ignoring, for the moment, the immortality that is in good fiction. Because, when all is said and done, it is not the dull fact, recorded in terms of historical truth, that is going to survive. If you wait long enough you will see in the end that historical fact, carefully checked up and audited by the historian, cedes place to the poet's embroidered lie.

In terms of one or other kind of sociological interpretation of history, there were potent economic factors underlying the events connected with Edgworth Hill and Naseby. But to a poet it is all a story about a princess and a crown under an oak tree and Rupert of the Rhine. And it is the poet's lying version that is accepted in the end. (This might not apply altogether exclusively at the present day, perhaps. But this is only because at the present moment we still have so many people in our midst with 19th century minds – writers who have not yet realised, as the scientists have done, that 19th century rationalism is out of date.)

I trust that the reader will forgive the above rather undignified commentary. It is rather difficult to write about ghosts and have your nerves completely steady at the same time. (And I have just thought of something else that was peculiar about that native cyclist on the Pretoria road.) The artist hasn't got any right to ridicule reason, when he himself has got all those other gifts. In the same way, I feel, sometimes, that it was an unworthy thing for Edgar Allan Poe to have written his sonnet "To Science" – when he had his own "summer dream beneath the tamarind tree". But somebody must have come and disturbed him there, like a man came and disturbed me, also, the other day. It was a man who spoke about Ecology (which I had never heard of) as though it was a highly important word. And I also thought that it was something important, at first. Because I didn't know how it was spelt, I imagined that he was talking about Echo-logy. And I thought it was very fine: something, I fancied, to do with the lore of echoes.

And an echo is very important. For the ghost is sister to the echo. An echo is music's phantom, sound's frail spectre.

And when I have walked near a graveyard at night, and I have found myself on the verge of getting panicky, thinking of ghosts, then I have been able to still my fears in a very simple fashion. For I have thought, "Are we not also but ghosts, all we human beings who wander on the earth? What are we who live, but ghosts who walk by day?" And I have sauntered past that cemetery in another sort of fear – in trepidation lest my presence should distress that other ghost that already haunts the tomb.

And when I would start running, afterwards, and fast too, grabbing tight onto my hat, it was just to let that ghost know that he hadn't got to worry about me at all.

I can see, now, that it is a good thing to be friendly with ghosts. A headless apparition in rusty mail and clanking armour; a slender shade trailing her diaphanous robes in a religious light; an ignorant kafir riding upside down on a push-bike.

Because, when you start feeling friendly towards ghosts it is by an easy transition that you begin entertaining amicable sentiments in regard to human beings also. And you start acquiring the right kind of humility. And I feel, reading his sonnet "To Science" again, that this is something Edgar Allan Poe should have learnt also. You haven't been given a superior intellect – or what you imagine is a superior intellect – merely in order that you should look down on somebody who has not got your gifts, and who in his simplicity talks about Ecology. Rather should you try and lift him up. The chances are that he has got qualities of sincerity and moral character that you will never have.

Very illuminating truths emerge from our contact with the ghosts. Next time I go down to the Cape I feel I must try to get a glimpse of Van der Decken, still trying to get his ship into Table Bay. He has been trying to do that for over 300 years now; the legend of the Flying Dutchman is that he used blasphemous language, and for that reason he isn't allowed to get his ship into port. I should imagine that by this time the way he is swearing must be something awful.

"Let the ghosts go," Ingersoll said. "We will worship them no more. Let them cover up their eyeless sockets with their fleshless hands and depart forever from the imagination of men."

But I can't agree with that. It is a very salutary thing to have ghosts about, enabling us to see ourselves and our fellow human beings as loitering "manes" also. This is always an important discovery to make. It is like when a convict, after he has served a long period of imprisonment, hears the prison gate clang shut behind him; and, walking out into the sunshine of the street, he realises for the first time that the whole world is a gaol.

And it is no doubt in recognition of this need that the men of olden time brought the great tidings of the Holy Ghost.

Playing Sane

I converse fairly regularly with a gentleman who was confined for a somewhat lengthy period in what was known in the old days as a lunatic asylum and is to-day called by the euphemistic appellation of a mental hospital.

"They are all balmy there," the gentleman informs me, "male nurses, schizophrenics, psychiatrists, paranoics, pathologists, homicidal maniacs, keepers and attendants." This statement did not strike me as being particularly novel, nor this ex-patient's assertions as to the strain that was imposed on him in his trying to preserve his mental balance in the almost constant company of mental specialists and asylum keepers.

The psychiatrists were very difficult, my informant states.

"There was one fat mental specialist with a queer glint in his eyes who kept on asking me if I heard voices. He meant when you hear voices and there aren't any. Well, I never heard voices. And if I did, I wouldn't have been mad enough to tell him. And every time I told him I didn't hear voices you should have seen the look of disappointment that came into his face. I had the uneasy feeling that he heard voices all day long, talking all kinds of blah to him, and why he wanted me to say I also heard those voices was so that he wouldn't feel so alone.

"I even got so, after a while, that I would sit for hours on end in my padded cell, just listening. I thought that if perhaps I could only hear one voice, just saying a few simple things to me, and I could repeat it to the psychiatrist, he would feel a lot better. But it just wouldn't work. During all the time that I was locked up in that madhouse I never once heard voices. And it wasn't from want of trying."

Thus spoke a former inmate of a mental hospital who was discharged, I suppose, on the grounds that he was incurable.

Now, this whole question of insanity, officially classified as such, raises a number of interesting problems, some of them insoluble, except, possibly, by a lunatic.

There is Edgar Allan Poe's story of a man's visit to an insane asylum. The visitor is taken round by a person whom he believes to be the doctor in charge of the institution, but who eventually turns out to be the chief lunatic, for there had taken place, unknown to the outside world, a lunatic's revolution at this establishment, with the result that the lunatics had taken the places of the medical men and the keepers, these latter being now kept in confinement under the surveillance of their former charges.

It is a gripping story. It is a story that has got everything. But what puzzled me at the time I read it, was the question as to how this substitution of authority was ever detected. I mean, how is it possible ever to tell?

I feel that a change-over of this description has taken place in many of the world's best asylums before to-day (you know how cunning lunatics are) and with nobody the wiser.

When once a change of this nature had taken place in the administration, it seems only too simple to keep the new regime in power for ever. Picture yourself as the visitor to this institution. The new superintendent (former head lunatic) shows you around.

The first patient he will confront you with, as a matter of course, will be the former superintendent.

"A very interesting case, this one," the new superintendent will inform you. "It's all frightfully intricate. We have diagnosed it as dementia praecox with diurgic aberrations of the left cranial tissues. It's a species of insanity that is mystifying Krafft-Ebing and Walters and other psychiatrists and schizophrenics who are making a special study of it."

At this stage, of course, the former superintendent will announce his identity, which will be just what the new superintendent wants in order to establish his point.

"You're mad," the former superintendent will announce to the man who has usurped his job. "In fact," – and he will try to approach the visitor confidentially, lowering his voice and looking knowingly at him – "in fact, they are all mad, here. I am really the superintendent. The lunatics have taken charge of the place here and have locked me up. I am busy writing to the Department of the Interior about it. You ought to see the copies I have got of all the letters I have written to the Department of the Interior. Stacks of letters and I get no answer. I am beginning to think that the Department of the Interior is also mad."

"Like I said to you," the new superintendent will announce to the visitor, "just about incorrigible. We give him all the pencils and paper he wants for writing. It takes his mind off things. But when once a man becomes graphomaniac, like he is, there isn't much hope for him."

You can go on this way *ad lib*. Because, in actual fact, you don't know where you are, in this world. It's a frightening thought. Take any book on psychopathology, written by almost any authority on abnormalities of the brain, either in its structure or its functions, and after a couple of paragraphs, if you know anything about the art of letters, you can feel to what an extent graphomania has been the dynamism that has impelled the author to sit down and write the book at all.

You will also discover, after the first couple of pages, that the writer is going to impart to you his own individual theories, which are completely different from any theories any other psychiatrist has ever held, and from then onwards the writer enters a realm of marvellously disconnected fantasy, where he can let himself go just as mad as he likes.

Something that I have also learnt from my ex-mental-hospital-inmate informant – and it is something that has shaken me – is the fact that the patients in mental institutions are no longer required to wear a distinctive garb. Now, in the old days it was different. The custom of making the patient wear a uniform decorated with stripes or squares or daisy-chains was very sensible. It gave you a good rough and ready idea as to who was who in a lunatic asylum. But to-day that has gone by the board. The present-day situation is one fraught with peril. In the rough and tumble of trying to establish, under prevailing conditions, who is the mental specialist and who the mental case requiring treatment, some pretty ghastly scenes must get enacted. And the strain, of course, is on the keepers.

The whole field of insanity is of absorbing importance at the present time. To all of us. It is enough if you have got a fixed stare in your eyes and you seem sure of what you are doing, for people to be impressed with you and to invest you with all the qualities of leadership. Human nature can't take in the idea that a man should look as mad as all that, and carry on in a mad fashion, and on top of all that actually be mad. It doesn't seem logical.

You can see this happening everywhere, and not only in the sphere of statesmanship. Where a man with a one-track insanity type of mind comes along, normal people instinctively stand aside. They accord him all due respect straight away. They can't believe that a man can have all that insane energy, and still be wrong.

In this respect we are all still very primitive. We stand in the same awe of energetic insanity as did any of the members of a primitive tribe. We are actually in a more dangerous position than are savages with their taboos and rigid caste systems – all aimed at keeping the lunatic out. We even go so far as to allow him to write treatises on psychopathology. This is a terrible thought.

As a result of all this, we civilised human beings are all caught up in a whirlpool of mental aberrations, our thoughts moulded in terms of chaos conceived by lunatics of both the past and the present. To take just a simple example. Almost every civilised person you come across will tell you that the earth isn't flat. It's round. It's like an orange. It is, to be still more technical, an oblate spheroid. And the authority he quotes for this is that some astronomer a few hundred years ago saw it all in a telescope. Copernicus, and he saw it all moving.

The point of all this, obviously enough, is that the earth is flat. And it doesn't move. These facts are so axiomatic that you don't even need to test them out for yourself. You have just got to look at the earth and see. And you can feel it doesn't move.

Our whole mental attitude towards life is hedged around with unrealities of this description. We live in a chaos of ideas thought out by cranks. We have been unable to protect our civilisation from the perilous invasion of the lunatic, whom we have been unable to keep out. The result to-day, when you reject insanity, and you depict things just as they are, and you see the sun as Phoebus, as Apollo, as Ra bestriding the heavens, and a red sky in the morning is the shepherd's warning, then it sounds as though you are trying to talk poetry. Whereas it is all just plain, factual stuff, based on simple observations and divest of insanity.

We all know the expression "playing mad". In this mad world there are, alas, a good many of us who have to engage in the pastime of "playing sane". There is quite a lot of fun in it. Playing sane-sane.

Climbing Table Mountain

There are a number of things that I have been wanting to do in Cape Town, and since I have not succeeded in accomplishing them I have, as a result, been overtaken by a singular sense of frustration.

For one thing, I have been wanting to climb Table Mountain. Consequently we set off, in a party of three, early one morning, in hiking shorts, and went by bus to Kloof Nek, where – we were informed – a footpath winds all the way round the back of the mountain to the Blinkwater Gorge, up which you climb to the summit. The bus was crowded, and so we had to go and sit on top. I hoped that the road up Table Mountain would not be equally crowded. I made the ascent to the upper deck of the bus with comparative ease. The first part of the climb wasn't so bad, I said to myself. The bus came to a halt at the Kloof Nek terminus and we alighted without incident.

It was very pleasant sauntering along the footpath that winds around the lower slopes of Table Mountain. Stately pines towered above us, their fragrance awakening a haunting nostalgia, their nearness affording me a subtle sense of comfort. I felt that a tree-trunk would be something substantial to hold on to, higher up the trail, should a sudden eventuality arise. But after a while I noticed that the pines were getting spaced out more and more. In the end, they gave out altogether. I looked up. For the rest of the way to the summit there seemed only rocks and kranse.

I could sense that the other two members of our little party shared this feeling of uneasiness at the thought of our having now climbed out above the pine belt. There was about it a finality that seemed almost like that of doom. But we didn't let on to each other what we really thought. We only said that we were glad that there were no more pines around to obscure the view. We also said that if we got no higher up the mountain than we were now – which was, of course, absurd – it would have been well worth it, just for the magnificent prospect that met our gaze when we sat down by the footpath, after we had passed the last of the trees.

Below us lay Camps Bay. The oblong area of grasslands fronting the sea was reduced to the size of a good-class magazine. Far out at sea, where the blue of sky and ocean blended, we discerned a full-rigged ship which we recognised immediately, by her broad square stern and old-fashioned mizzen-sails, as the Flying Dutchman (captain, Mr. Van der Decken). We felt highly privileged at being able to view, even across so great a distance, that ancient Dutch East Indiaman, long celebrated in legend and song. We watched the ship until she disappeared below the horizon. Once again, in the course of two centuries of beating off the Cape of Storms, Van der Decken had failed to make the harbour. We had sort of imagined that he would fail.

We proceeded on our way. After a while we reached a signpost pointing silently and steeply upwards. It read: "Blinkwater Ravine – Blinkwaterkloof." In neither official language did that precipitous piece of direction sound particularly heartening. But that, clearly, was the way we had to go. Very reluctantly we left our well-trodden little footpath and started scrambling over rocks and shrubbery, onwards and upwards, following the way the signpost pointed. We were no longer skirting the lower slopes of the Lion's Rump. We were climbing Table Mountain in earnest. We thrilled to this knowledge. It was very exciting. At the same time – speaking strictly for myself, personally – I was conscious of a certain measure of trepidation.

The mountain towered in vast bulk above us. Below was a steep and empty desolation. The green of Camps Bay had dwindled to the size of a postage stamp. Van der Decken's ship was no longer there to cheer us up.

But we didn't let on to each other what we really felt.

It was getting on well towards midday, when, keeping as much to the left as we could we found ourselves very high up and right inside the shadows of the kloof. It was chilly and we shivered. In whichever direction we looked, we saw the world bathed in brilliant sunshine. We alone, clambering upwards towards the top of the gorge, were in deep shadow. This thought made us shiver still more.

We could see that we had climbed a very long way, and we were very pleased with the effort we had made. The green of Camps Bay had disappeared altogether, but in front of us there stretched, extending into the infinite distance, an expanse of sea and sky and burning coastline that must remain as one of the most majestic sights on which it is possible for the gaze of man to rest. We could see clear out beyond Hout Bay and Slangkop to that lonely spot in the world where the Atlantic and Indian Oceans meet. Even to the untrained eye the line of demarcation between these two giant oceans is easily discernible. It is a thick straight line that looks as though it was drawn with a ruler. The Atlantic Ocean, on one side of this line, has got more of a cobalt tinge in its waters, while the Indian Ocean, on the other side of it, is more wavy, sort of. I don't know how deep down that line goes, but it must be a good number of fathoms, by the look of it.

After we had rested on the dizzy ledge for a while we embarked by common accord and without any one of us having to make the suggestion, on the descent of Table Mountain. Getting down was easy. We sat well back and used our hands and feet only as brakes on our progress, when we appeared to be making the descent too quickly, and in order to circumvent jagged rock faces. But we adhered to our policy of resting at intervals. And on at least three occasions we had the satisfaction of being able to call out useful instructions to parties of climbers who passed near us on their way up. We were in high good spirits and did not admit – certainly not to each other – that we had turned back before we had reached the summit of Table Mountain. By the late afternoon we had got so far down the mountain-side that the green oblong of Camps Bay was again of substantial size, and when we caught another glimpse, in the westering sun, of Van der Decken's Flying Dutchman, coming back again over the horizon and with all sails set for Table Bay, we could have laughed to kill ourselves. We just knew he wouldn't make it.

Quite a number of people passed us that afternoon, all of them on their way up, along Blinkwater Gorge, to the top of Table Mountain. One of them was a woman pushing a pram.

126

Marico Revisited

A month ago I revisited the Marico Bushveld, a district in the Transvaal to which I was sent, a long time ago, as a schoolteacher, and about which part of the country I have written, in the years that followed, a number of simple stories which I believe, in all modesty, are not without a certain degree of literary merit.

There were features about the Marico Bushveld that were almost too gaudy. That part of the country had been practically derelict since the Boer War and the rinderpest. Many of the farms north of the Dwarsberge had been occupied little more than ten years before by farmers who had trekked into the Marico from the Northern Cape and the Western Transvaal. The farmers there were real Boers. I am told that I have a deep insight into the character of the Afrikaner who lives his life on the platteland. I acquired this knowledge in the Marico, where I was sent when my mind was most open to impressions.

Then there was the bush. Thorn-trees. Withaaks and kameeldorings. The kremetart-boom. Swarthaak and blinkblaar and wag-'n-bietjie. Moepels and maroelas. The sunbaked vlakte and the thorn-tree and South Africa. Trees are more than vegetation and more than symbols and more than pallid sentimentality, of the order of "Woodman, spare that tree," or "Poems are made by fools like me." Nevertheless, what the oak and the ash and the cypress are to Europe, the thorn-tree is to South Africa. And if laurel and myrtle and bay are for chaplet and wreath, thorns are for a crown.

The bush was populated with koedoes and cows and duikers and steenbokkies and oxen and gemsbok and donkeys and occasional leopards. There were also ribbokke in the kranse, and green and brown mambas, of which hair-raising stories were told, and mules that were used to pull carts because it was an unhealthy area for horses. Mules were also used for telling hair-raising stories about.

And the sunsets in the Marico Bushveld are incredible things, heavily striped like prison bars and flamboyant like their kafir blankets.

Then there were boreholes, hundreds of feet deep, from which water had to be pumped by hand into the cattle-troughs in times of drought. And there was a Bechuana chief who had once been to London, where he had been received in audience by His Majesty, George V, a former English king; and when, on departing from Buckingham Palace, he had been questioned by the High Commissioner as to what form the conversation had taken, he had replied, very simply, this Bechuana chief, "We kings know what to discuss."

There were occasional visits from Dutch Reformed Church predikants. And a few meetings of the Dwarsberg Debatsvereniging. And there were several local feuds. For I was to find that while the bush was of infinite extent, and the farms very many miles apart, the paths through the thorn-trees were narrow.

It was to this part of the country, the northern section of the Marico Bushveld, where the Transvaal ends and the Bechuanaland Protectorate begins, that I returned for a brief visit after an absence of many years. And I found, what I should have known all along, of course, that it was the present that was haunted, and that the past was not full of ghosts. The phantoms are what you carry around with you, in your head, like you carry dreams under your arm.

And when you revisit old scenes it is yourself as you were in the past, that you encounter, and if you are in love with yourself, – as everybody should be in love with himself, since it is only in that way, as Christ pointed out, that a man can love his neighbour – then there is a sweet sadness in a meeting of this description. There is the gentle melancholy of the twilight, dark eyes in faces upturned in a trancelike pallor. And fragrances. And thoughts like soft rain falling on old tomb-stones.

And on the train that night on my way back to the Bushveld, I came across a soldier who said to me, "As soon as I am out of this uniform I am going back to cattle-smuggling."

128

These words thrilled me. A number of my stories have dealt with the time-honoured Marico custom of smuggling cattle across the frontier of the Bechuanaland Protectorate. So I asked whether cattle-smuggling still went on. "More than ever," the soldier informed me. He looked out of the train window into the dark, "And I'll tell you that at this moment, as I am sitting here talking to you, there is somebody bringing in cattle through the wire."

I was very glad to hear this. I was glad to find that the only part of my stories that could have dated had not done so. It is only things indirectly connected with economics that can change. Droughts and human nature don't.

Next morning we were in Mafeking. Mafeking is outside the Transvaal. It is about twenty miles inside the borders of the Northern Cape. And to proceed to Ramoutsa, a native village in the Bechuanaland Protectorate which is the nearest point on the railway line to the part of the Groot Marico to which we wanted to go, we had first to get a permit from the immigration official in Mafeking. All this seemed very confusing, somehow. We merely wanted to travel from Johannesburg to an area in the North-Western Transvaal, and in order to get there it turned out that we had first to cross into the Cape Province, and that from the Cape we had to travel through the Bechuanaland Protectorate, which is a Crown Colony, and which you can't enter until an immigration official has first telephoned Pretoria about it.

We reached Ramoutsa late in the afternoon.

From there we travelled to the Marico by car. Within the hour we had crossed the border into the Transvaal. We were once more on Transvaal soil, for which we were, naturally, homesick, having been exiles in foreign parts from since early morning. So the moment we crossed the barbed-wire fence separating the Bechuanaland Protectorate from the Marico we stopped the car and got out on to the veld. We said it was fine to set foot on Transvaal soil once more. And we also said that while it was a good thing to travel through foreign countries, which we had been doing since six o'clock that morning, and that foreign travel had a broadening effect on the mind, we were glad that our heads had not been turned by these experiences, and that we had not permitted ourselves to be influenced by alien modes of life and thought.

We travelled on through the bush over stony paths that were little more than tracks going in between the trees and underneath their branches, the thorns tearing at the windscreen and the hood of the car in the same way as they had done years before, when I had first visited the Marico. I was glad to find that nothing had changed.

Dusk found us in the shadow of the Dwarsberge, not far from our destination, and we came across a spot on the veld that I recognised. It was one of the stations at which the bi-weekly Government lorry from Zeerust stopped on its way up towards the Limpopo. How the lorry drivers knew that this place was a station, years ago, was through the presence of a large anthill, into the crest of which a pair of koedoe antlers had been thrust. That spot had not changed. The anthill was still surmounted by what looked like that same pair of koedoe horns. The station had not grown perceptibly in the intervening years. The only sign of progress was that, in addition to the horns on its summit, the anthill was further decorated with a rusty milk-can the bottom of which had been knocked out.

And so I arrived back in that part of the country to which the Transvaal Education Department in its wisdom had sent me years before. There is no other place I know that is so heavy with atmosphere, so strangely and darkly impregnated with that stuff of life that bears the authentic stamp of South Africa.

When I first went to the Marico it was in that season when the moepels were nearly ripening. And when I returned, years later, it was to find that the moepels in the Marico were beginning to ripen again.

FROM *Unto Dust* (1963)

Unto Dust

I have noticed that when a young man or woman dies, people get the feeling that there is something beautiful and touching in the event, and that it is different from the death of an old person. In the thought, say, of a girl of twenty sinking into an untimely grave, there is a sweet wistfulness that makes people talk all kinds of romantic words. She died, they say, young, she that was so full of life and so fair. She was a flower that withered before it bloomed, they say, and it all seems so fitting and beautiful that there is a good deal of resentment, at the funeral, over the crude questions that a couple of men in plain clothes from the landdrost's office are asking about cattle-dip.

But when you have grown old, nobody is very much interested in the manner of your dying. Nobody except you yourself, that is. And I think that your past life has got a lot to do with the way you feel when you get near the end of your days. I remember how, when he was lying on his death-bed, Andries Wessels kept on telling us that it was because of the blameless path he had trodden from his earliest years that he could compose himself in peace to lay down his burdens. And I certainly never saw a man breathe his last more tranquilly, seeing that right up to the end he kept on murmuring to us how happy he was, with heavenly hosts and invisible choirs of angels all around him.

Just before he died, he told us that the angels had even become visible. They were medium-sized angels, he said, and they had cloven hoofs and carried forks. It was obvious that Andries Wessels's ideas were getting a bit confused by then, but all the same I never saw a man die in a more hallowed sort of calm.

Once, during the malaria season in the Eastern Transvaal, it seemed to me, when I was in a high fever and like to die, that the whole world was a big burial-ground. I thought it was the earth itself that was a grave-yard, and not just those little fenced-in bits of land dotted with tombstones, in the shade of a Western Province oak tree or by the side of a Transvaal koppie. This was a nightmare that worried me a great deal, and so I was very glad, when I recovered from the fever, to think that we Boers had properly marked-out places on our farms for white people to be laid to rest in, in a civilised Christian way, instead of having to be buried just anyhow, along with a dead wild-cat, maybe, or a Bushman with a claypot, and things.

When I mentioned this to my friend, Stoffel Oosthuizen, who was in the Low Country with me at the time, he agreed with me wholeheartedly. There were people who talked in a high-flown way of death as the great leveller, he said, and those high-flown people also declared that everyone was made kin by death. He would still like to see those things proved, Stoffel Oosthuizen said. After all, that was one of the reasons why the Boers trekked away into the Transvaal and the Free State, he said, because the British Government wanted to give the vote to any Cape Coloured person walking about with a *kroes* head and big cracks in his feet.

The first time he heard that sort of talk about death coming to all of us alike, and making us all equal, Stoffel Oosthuizen's suspicions were aroused. It sounded like out of a speech made by one of those liberal Cape politicians, he explained.

I found something very comforting in Stoffel Oosthuizen's words.

Then, to illustrate his contention, Stoffel Oosthuizen told me a story of an incident that took place in a bygone Transvaal Kafir War. I don't know whether he told the story incorrectly, or whether it was just that kind of story, but, by the time he had finished, all my uncertainties had, I discovered, come back to me.

"You can go and look at Hans Welman's tombstone any time you are at Nietverdiend," Stoffel Oosthuizen said. "The slab of red sandstone is weathered by now, of course, seeing how long ago it all happened. But the inscription is still legible. I was with Hans Welman on that morning when he fell. Our commando had been ambushed by the kafirs and was retreating. I could do nothing for Hans Welman. Once, when I looked round, I saw a tall kafir bending over him and plunging an assegai into him. Shortly afterwards I saw the kafir stripping the clothes off Hans Welman. A yellow kafir dog was yelping excitedly around his black master. Although I was in grave danger myself, with several dozen kafirs making straight for me on foot through the bush, the fury I felt at the sight of what that tall kafir was doing made me hazard a last shot. Reining in my horse, and taking what aim I could under the circumstances, I pressed the trigger. My luck was in. I saw the kafir fall forward beside the naked body of Hans Welman. Then I set spurs to my horse and galloped off at full speed, with the foremost of my pursuers already almost upon me. The last I saw was that yellow dog bounding up to his master – whom I had wounded mortally, as we were to discover later.

"As you know, that kafir war dragged on for a long time. There were few pitched battles. Mainly, what took place were bush skirmishes, like the one in which Hans Welman lost his life.

"After about six months, quiet of a sort was restored to the Marico and Zoutpansberg districts. Then the day came when I went out, in company of a handful of other burghers, to fetch in the remains of Hans Welman, at his widow's request, for burial in the little cemetery plot on the farm. We took a coffin with us on a Cape cart.

"We located the scene of the skirmish without difficulty. Indeed, Hans Welman had been killed not very far from his own farm, which had been temporarily abandoned, together with the other farms in that part, during the time that the trouble with the kafirs had lasted. We drove up to the spot where I remembered having seen Hans Welman lying dead on the ground, with the tall kafir next to him. From a distance I again saw that yellow dog. He slipped away into the bush at our approach. I could not help feeling that there was something rather stirring about that beast's fidelity, even though it was bestowed on a dead kafir.

"We were now confronted with a queer situation. We found that what was left of Hans Welman and the kafir consisted of little more than pieces of sun-dried flesh and the dismembered fragments of bleached skeletons. The sun and wild animals and birds of prey had done their work. There was a heap of human bones, with here and there leathery strips of blackened flesh. But we could not tell which was the white man and which the kafir. To make it still more confusing, a lot of bones were missing alto-

gether, having no doubt been dragged away by wild animals into
their lairs in the bush. Another thing was that Hans Welman and
the kafir had been just about the same size."

Stoffel Oosthuizen paused in his narrative, and I let my imagination dwell for a moment on that situation. And I realised just how
those Boers must have felt about it: about the thought of bringing
the remains of a Transvaal burgher home to his widow for Christian burial, and perhaps having a lot of kafir bones mixed up with
the burgher – lying with him in the same tomb on which the
mauve petals from the oleander overhead would fall.

"I remember one of our party saying that that was the worst of
these kafir wars," Stoffel Oosthuizen continued. "If it had been a
war against the English, and part of a dead Englishman had got
lifted into that coffin by mistake, it wouldn't have mattered so
much," he said.

There seemed to me in this story to be something as strange as
the African veld. Stoffel Oosthuizen said that the little party of
Boers spent almost a whole afternoon with the remains in order
to try to get the white man sorted out from the kafir. By the evening they had laid all they could find of what seemed like Hans Welman's bones in the coffin in the Cape cart. The rest of the bones
and flesh they buried on the spot.

Stoffel Oosthuizen added that, no matter what the difference in
the colour of their skin had been, it was impossible to say that the
kafir's bones were less white than Hans Welman's. Nor was it possible to say that the kafir's sun-dried flesh was any blacker than the
white man's. Alive, you couldn't go wrong in distinguishing between a white man and a kafir. Dead, you had great difficulty in
telling them apart.

"Naturally, we burghers felt very bitter about this whole affair,"
Stoffel Oosthuizen said, "and our resentment was something that
we couldn't explain, quite. Afterwards, several other men who
were there that day told me that they had the same feelings of
suppressed anger that I did. They wanted somebody – just once –
to make a remark such as 'in death they were not divided'. Then
you would have seen an outburst all right. Nobody did say anything like that, however. We all knew better. Two days later a
funeral service was conducted in the little cemetery on the Wel-

man farm, and shortly afterwards the sandstone memorial was erected that you can still see there."

That was the story Stoffel Oosthuizen told me after I had recovered from the fever. It was a story that, as I have said, had in it features as strange as the African veld. But it brought me no peace in my broodings after that attack of malaria. Especially when Stoffel Oosthuizen spoke of how he had occasion, one clear night when the stars shone, to pass that quiet graveyard on the Welman farm. Something leapt up from the mound beside the sandstone slab. It gave him quite a turn, Stoffel Oosthuizen said, for the third time – and in that way – to come across that yellow kafir dog.

Dopper and Papist

It was a cold night (oom Schalk Lourens said) on which we drove with Gert Bekker in his Cape cart to Zeerust. I sat in front, next to Gert, who was driving. In the back seat were the predikant, Rev. Vermooten, and his ouderling, Isak Erasmus, who were on their way to Pretoria for the meeting of the Synod of the Dutch Reformed Church. The predikant was lean and hawk-faced; the ouderling was fat and had broad shoulders.

Gert Bekker and I did not speak. We had been transport-drivers together in our time, and we had learnt that when it is two men alone, travelling over a long distance, it is best to use few words, and those well-chosen. Two men, alone in each other's company, understand each other better the less they speak.

The horses kept up a good, steady trot. The lantern, swinging from side to side with the jogging of the cart, lit up stray patches of the uneven road and made bulky shadows rise up among the thorn-trees. In the back seat the predikant and the ouderling were discussing theology.

"You never saw such a lot of brandsiek sheep in your life," the predikant was saying, "as what Chris Haasbroek brought along as tithe."

We then came to a stony part of the road, and so I did not hear the ouderling's reply; but afterwards, above the rattling of the cart-wheels, I caught other snatches of God-fearing conversation, to do with the raising of pew-rents.

From there the predikant started discussing the proselytising activities being carried on among the local Bapedi kafirs by the Catholic mission at Vleisfontein. The predikant dwelt particularly on the ignorance of the Bapedi tribes and on the idolatrous form of the Papist Communion service, which was quite different from the Protestant Nagmaal, the predikant said, although to a Bapedi, walking with his buttocks sticking out, the two services might, perhaps, seem somewhat alike.

Rev. Vermooten was very eloquent when he came to denouncing the heresies of Catholicism. And he spoke loudly, so that we could hear him on the front seat. And I know that both Gert Bekker and I felt very good, then, deep inside us, to think that we were Protestants. The coldness of the night and the pale flickering of the lantern-light among the thorn-trees gave an added solemnity to the predikant's words.

I felt that it might perhaps be all right to be a Catholic if you were walking on a Zeerust side-walk in broad daylight, say. But it was a different matter to be driving through the middle of the bush on a dark night, with just a swinging lantern fastened to the side of a Cape cart with baling-wire. If the lantern went out suddenly, and you were left in the loneliest part of the bush, striking matches, then it must be a very frightening thing to be a Catholic, I thought.

This led me to thinking of Piet Reilly and his family, who were Afrikaners, like you and me, except that they were Catholics. Piet Reilly even brought out his vote for General Lemmer at the last Volksraad election, which we thought would make it unlucky for our candidate. But General Lemmer said no, he didn't mind how many Catholics voted for him. A Catholic's vote was, naturally not as good as a Dopper's, he said, but the little cross that had to be made behind a candidate's name cast out the evil that was of course otherwise lurking in a Catholic's ballot paper. And General Lemmer must have been right, because he got elected, that time.

While I was thinking on those lines, it suddenly struck me that Piet Reilly was now living on a farm about six miles on the bushveld side of Sephton's Nek, and that we would be passing his farm-house, which was near the road, just before daybreak. It was comforting to think that we would have the predikant and the ouderling in the Cape cart with us, when we passed the homestead of Piet Reilly, a Catholic, in the dark.

I tried to hear what the predikant was saying, in the back seat, to the ouderling. But the predikant was once more dealing with an abstruse point of religion, and had lowered his voice accordingly. I could catch only fragments of the ouderling's replies.

"Yes, dominee," I heard the ouderling affirm, "you are quite right. If he again tries to overlook your son for the job of anthrax inspector, then you must make it clear to the Chairman of the Board that you have all that information about his private life . . ."

I realised then that you could find much useful guidance for your everyday problems in the conversation of holy men.

The night got colder and darker.

The palm of my hand, pressed tight around the bowl of my pipe, was the only part of me that felt warm. My teeth began to chatter. I wished that, next time we stopped to let the horses blow, we could light a fire and boil coffee. But I knew that there was no coffee left in the chest under the back seat.

While I sat silent next to Gert Bekker, I continued to think of Piet Reilly and his wife and children. With Piet, of course, I could understand it. He himself had merely kept up the religion – if you could call what the Catholics believe in a religion – that he had inherited from his father and his grandfather. But there was Piet Reilly's wife, Gertruida, now. She had been brought up a respectable Dopper girl. She was one of the Drogedal Bekkers, and was, in fact, distantly related to Gert Bekker, who was sitting on the Cape cart next to me. There was something for you to ponder about, I thought to myself, with the cold all the time looking for new places in my skin through which to strike into my bones.

The moment Gertruida met Piet Reilly she forgot all about the sacred truths she had learnt at her mother's knee. And on the day she got married she was saying prayers to the Virgin Mary on a string of beads, and was wearing a silver cross at her throat that was as soft and white as the roses she held pressed against her. Here was now a sweet Dopper girl turned Papist.

As I have said, I knew that there was no coffee left in the box under the back seat; but I did know that under the front seat there was a full bottle of raw peach brandy. In fact, I could see the neck of the bottle protruding from between Gert Bekker's ankles.

I also knew, through all the years of transport-driving that we had done together, that Gert Bekker had already, over many miles of road, been thinking how we could get the cork off the bottle without the predikant and the ouderling shaking their heads reprovingly. And the way he managed it in the end was, I thought, highly intelligent.

For, when he stopped the cart again to rest the horses, he alighted beside the road and held out the bottle to our full view.

"There is brandy in this bottle, dominie," Gert Bekker said to the predikant, "that I keep for the sake of the horses on cold nights, like now. It is an old Marico remedy for when horses are in danger of getting the *floute,* I take a few mouthfuls of the brandy, which I then blow into the nostrils of the horses, who don't feel the cold so much, after that. The brandy revives them."

Gert commenced blowing brandy into the face of the horse on the near side, to show us.

Then he beckoned to me, and I also alighted and went and stood next to him, taking turns with him in blowing brandy into the eyes and nostrils of the offside horse. We did this several times.

The predikant asked various questions, to show how interested he was in this old-fashioned method of over-coming fatigue in draught-animals. But what the predikant said at the next stop made me perceive that he was more than a match for a dozen men like Gert Bekker in point of astuteness.

When we stopped the cart, the predikant held up his hand.

"Don't you and your friend trouble to get off this time," the predikant called out when Gert Bekker was once more reaching for the bottle, "the ouderling and I have decided to take turns with you in blowing brandy into the horses' faces. We don't want to put all the hard work on to your shoulders."

We made several more halts after that, with the result that daybreak found us still a long way from Sephton's Nek. In the early dawn we saw the thatched roof of Piet Reilly's house through the thorn-trees some distance from the road. When the predikant suggested that we call at the homestead for coffee, we explained to him that the Reillys were Catholics.

"But isn't Piet Reilly's wife a relative of yours?" the predikant asked of Gert Bekker. "Isn't she your second-cousin, or something?"

"They are Catholics," Gert answered.

"Coffee," the predikant insisted.

"Catholics," Gert Bekker repeated stolidly.

The upshot of it was, naturally enough, that we outspanned

shortly afterwards in front of the Reilly homestead. That was the kind of man that the predikant was in an argument.

"The coffee will be ready soon," the predikant said as we walked up to the front door. "There is smoke coming out of the chimney."

Almost before we had stopped knocking, Gertruida Reilly had opened both the top and bottom doors. She started slightly when she saw, standing in front of her, a minister of the Dutch Reformed Church. In spite of her look of agitation, Gertruida was still pretty, I thought, after ten years of being married to Piet Reilly.

When she stepped forward to kiss her cousin, Gert Bekker, I saw him turn away, sadly; and I realised something of the shame that she had brought on her whole family through her marriage to a Catholic.

"You looked startled when you saw me, Gertruida," the predikant said, calling her by her first name, as though she was still a member of his congregation.

"Yes," Gertruida answered. "Yes – I was – surprised."

"I suppose it was a Catholic priest that you wanted to come to your front door," Gert Bekker said, sarcastically. Yet there was a tone in his voice that was not altogether unfriendly.

"Indeed, I was expecting a Catholic priest," Gertruida said, leading us into the voorkamer. "But if the Lord has sent the dominie and his ouderling, instead, I am sure it will be well, also."

It was only then, after she had explained to us what had happened, that we understood why Gertruida was looking so troubled. Her eight-year-old daughter had been bitten by a snake; they couldn't tell from the fang-marks if it was a ringhals or a bakkop. Piet Reilly had driven off in the mule-cart to Vleisfontein, the Catholic Mission Station, for a priest.

They had cut open and cauterised the wound and had applied red permanganate. The rest was a matter for God. And that was why, when she saw the predikant and the ouderling at her front door, Gertruida believed that the Lord had sent them.

I was glad that Gert Bekker did not at that moment think of mentioning that we had really come for coffee.

"Certainly, I shall pray for your little girl's recovery," the predikant said to Gertruida. "Take me to her."

Gertruida hesitated.

"Will you – will you pray for her the Catholic way, dominie?" Gertruida asked.

Now it was the predikant's turn to draw back.

"But, Gertruida," he said, "you, you whom I myself confirmed in the Enkel-Gereformeerde Kerk in Zeerust – how can you now ask me such a thing? Did you not learn in the catechism that the Romish ritual is a mockery of the Holy Ghost?"

"I married Piet Reilly," Gertruida answered simply, "and his faith is my faith. Piet has been very good to me, Father. And I love him."

We noticed that Gertruida called the predikant "Father," now, and not "Dominie." During the silence that followed, I glanced at the candle burning before an image of the Mother Mary in a corner of the voorkamer. I looked away quickly from that unrighteousness.

The predikant's next words took us by complete surprise.

"Have you got some kind of a prayer-book," the predikant asked, "that sets out the – the Catholic form for a . . ."

"I'll fetch it from the other room," Gertruida answered.

When she had left, the predikant tried to put our minds at ease.

"I am only doing this to help a mother in distress," he explained to the ouderling. "It is something that the Lord will understand. Gertruida was brought up a Dopper girl. In some ways she is still one of us. She does not understand that I have no authority to conduct this Catholic service for the sick."

The ouderling was going to say something.

But at that moment Gertruida returned with a little black book that you could almost have taken for a Dutch Reformed Church psalm-book. Only, I knew that what was printed inside it was as iniquitous as the candle burning in the corner.

Yet I also began to wonder if, in not knowing the difference, a Bapedi really was so very ignorant, even though he walked with his buttocks sticking out.

"My daughter is in this other room," Gertruida said, and started in the direction of the door. The predikant followed her. Just before entering the bedroom he turned round and faced the ouderling.

"Will you enter with me, Brother Erasmus?" the predikant asked.

The ouderling did not answer. The veins stood out on his forehead. On his face you could read the conflict that went on inside him. For what seemed a very long time he stood quite motionless. Then he stooped down to the rusbank for his hat – which he did not need – and walked after the predikant into the bedroom.

My First Love

It was when I visited the de Bruyns of Drogedal that I saw Lettie de Bruyn for the first time: in the sense that I saw her properly, I mean. I was then nearly twenty, and Lettie must have been somewhere between sixteen and seventeen. It was long since I had last visited the Drogedal area, for this region was not situated on the main road to Zeerust, but was connected with the outside world by a dusty little side-road that wound along the side of Paradys Kop. Thus I noticed a few changes that had taken place there since my last visit.

I drove the new teacher to Drogedal in the mule-cart so that he could visit the de Bruyn and Bekker families who lived somewhat isolatedly below the Paradys Kop. A considerable number of children from Drogedal attended the Heimweeberg School where the Transvaal Education Department had just appointed Mr. Herklaas Huysmans as the new headmaster. Although he was only a year or two older than I was, I always addressed him as "Mr. Huysmans." There was something dignified about his appearance that prevented me from calling him bluntly "neef Herklaas." (Months later I thought out a whole lot of other names for him.)

The official position filled by Mr. Huysmans was of a highly responsible nature, for he was not only the principal of that little bushveld school, he was the whole school staff as well. He boarded with us on our farm, and my father was very pleased about this and urged me to spend as much time as possible in his company. My father maintained that it was of great educational value to me to associate with a school principal, seeing that I had only a little book learning.

I thought that my father, who during his whole life had only been to school for six months, would derive more benefit than I from Mr. Huysmans's company. However, I did not express my opinion. For I still lived with my parents, and my father was a man with the highest learning in the Marico as regards the handling of a short piece of undressed oxhide.

One Saturday, after we had eaten our midday meal and before we had pushed our chairs back, Mr. Huysmans informed us that he should like that afternoon to visit the Bekkers and de Bruyns. They were the only families with children at Heimweeberg School whom he had not yet visited.

"The Education Department requires that I visit each pupil at his home once a term," the principal explained, while he looked straight at me to suggest that it was time for me to run out and harness the mules.

"Yes, my son Schalk can take you over there," said my father in his obliging way. "It will be of educational value for Schalk, as well as, perhaps, dusty and hot on that road at this time of the day."

"But we're having a shooting contest at Derdepoort this afternoon . . ." I began to explain. But just at that moment my father made a gruff noise, which helped me immediately to see that my father was right, and that it was necessary for me to acquire further book knowledge. As a result the mules were harnessed and Mr. Huysmans and I were on the way to Drogedal in no time.

"Did the headmaster who was here before me visit the Drogedal families regularly?" Mr. Huysmans wanted to know after we had been on the road for about an hour and a half in the open mule-cart, while the sun burnt steadily down on our necks.

"No, not exactly," I answered.

"I can well believe that," said Mr. Huysmans meaningfully while perspiration poured from him.

For the last few miles the school-master complained continuously about the dust and the heat and the horse-flies. Nevertheless I preferred that to the instructive sort of talks he was sometimes in the habit of giving. Since he was the cause of my not being able to attend the shooting contest at Derdepoort, it would have been unbearable to me if on top of that I still had to listen to an educational little talk about how many square Cape roods there are in a morgen.

At last we reached our destination.

"There are several Bekker and de Bruyn families living out here in the backveld," I explained as the cart turned the last bend.

146

"Yes, and look, here now is Gys Bekker's place. That mud-coloured bit of wall sticking out between those two heaps. As you know, the Bekkers and de Bruyns have quite a number of children who go to school, but the people here are just slightly – how should I say? – conservative. Ah! now you can see Gys Bekker's house better. That is his dining-room – look, where that plump young Friesland bullock is coming out. And that woman with the wash-rag who is now coming after that bullock is Gys Bekker's . . ."

Just then the school-master interrupted me with the proposal that we should rather go and look up a few de Bruyn families. The Bekkers seemed, after all, slightly too conservative, the school-master explained.

So it happened that later that afternoon we sat and drank coffee in Arnoldus de Bruyn's voorkamer. I have mentioned already the changes that were to be seen there. Arnoldus de Bruyn had, for example, fitted the voorkamer with a wooden ceiling. He had also laid out a front stoep of blue slate-stone, and had put up a wire fence with a green gate, with the result that even the stupidest sort of fat calf would have to think twice before taking Arnoldus's voorkamer for the place where there was the manger with the cut-up sheaves.

I began to chat with Arnoldus de Bruyn about the improvements he had brought about. I sat on the riempie-bottomed bench next to Mr. Huysmans. Oom Arnoldus sat opposite us and puffed clouds of blue smoke up towards the ceiling – of which you could see he was very proud. His wife and a few older children also sat with us in the voorhuis.

I felt that compliment was called for.

"Oom Arnoldus, you've really altered your house nicely," I said. "At least your house no longer looks so very much like a stable. What I mean is, who ever saw a cowshed with striped curtains in front of the window?"

Although I should have preferred to have expressed myself more skilfully, Arnoldus was highly pleased with my little speech and smiled in a satisfied sort of way. My reference to Arnoldus de Bruyn's place gave rise, at any rate, to a detailed discussion by the school-master of the subject "The Dwellings of the Peoples of Distant Lands." He ended with a description of the houses of the

147

Eskimoes which they build of ice. Arnoldus de Bruyn shook his head thoughtfully over this and said: "Well, well – what won't people think of next!"

In the meantime I had taken a proper look at Lettie de Bruyn. She was another one of the changes I have spoken of. At any rate, she seemed to be very different from when we were children together. What especially surprised me was that she seemed so calm now. She had also grown tall: something I noticed when she approached the riempie bench to serve me and the school-master with coffee.

When I helped myself to sugar I spilled half my coffee in my saucer.

I wanted to chat a little with Lettie de Bruyn about our childhood years, but my tongue wouldn't come loose. Even in taking my second cup of coffee – which I also partly spilled, this time over the school-master's trouser-leg – I couldn't find any words.

The following Saturday I again drove Mr. Huysmans over to Drogedal. He said that it was his duty to visit the families there, seeing that they had become so conservative simply because they had not had enough elevating company. Nevertheless, it was peculiar to me that on every one of the following Saturdays, when I drove Mr. Huysmans to Drogedal, he only visited the home of Arnoldus de Bruyn. He closed his eyes completely to the other de Bruyn families, and as far as the Bekkers were concerned, it was clear that he wouldn't have been much perturbed if they had grown more conservative by the day.

Naturally I did not mind. I could never scrape up enough courage to address a word directly to Lettie de Bruyn, but I did progress so far as to lay my hand lightly on hers (after I had first put my cup down) each time she came and stood in front of me with the tray. She always blushed. It moved me to think how much the two of us could say to each other, Lettie de Bruyn and I, without using words – and without even needing much learning for it either.

Mr. Huysmans spoke in his most elevating manner about how envious other teachers were of him, because he was so talented.

"A colleague of mine even said out of jealousy," Mr. Huysmans declared, "that the Department sent me here because I am useless."

148

I winked at Lettie when the teacher spoke like that. She smiled back.

So you can imagine how shocked I was on the morning Mr. Huysmans, all-innocently, announced to my parents that he would no longer impose on them at our house over the week-ends, since he intended henceforth to ride on the school wagon to Drogedal every Friday afternoon and stay over until Monday morning at the de Bruyns'.

From then on until the end of the school-term we no longer saw Mr. Huysmans at our farm during the week-ends. And I could think of no excuse for visiting Drogedal. There was no way by which I could communicate with Lettie de Bruyn.

I am certain that none of the pupils of Heimweeberg School could have longed for the end of that school-term as much as I, whose school-days were already so far behind me.

But at last the schools did break up. Mr. Huysmans went to Pretoria to spend the holidays there with his parents. The Marico Boers inspanned their ox-wagons and took the road to Zeerust in order to attend the Nagmaal. And thus I knew where I would again meet Lettie de Bruyn.

It was with the inevitability of something that happens in a dream that Lettie de Bruyn came to me, in a night of summer fragrances, when the stars glistened hugely.

This time, also, we still did not speak. By an arrangement which we had made without the use of words, she slipped out of the veld-tent that Arnoldus de Bruyn had pitched on the church square, to come and meet me. She was wearing a long white dress, and when she came near to me I saw how tall and thin she was, and how pale her cheeks were – white, like her dress. When I stretched out my arms she withdrew herself playfully. I chased her. But when I caught up with her and laughing took her into my arms, she suddenly turned her face away. Before I could grasp what was happening, I let her slip out of my arms again. It all had the feeling of a dream.

The suddenness of her movements took me by surprise, and before I could collect myself again she suddenly pressed her mouth against my cheek. Then she ran into the shadows, to the tent where her parents and brothers and sisters were sleeping.

I knew that she would come to me again the next night.

What troubled me was the realisation that lately Lettie de Bruyn had learnt too much. Undoubtedly she had been learning during the school-term that had just ended. I walked through the deserted streets of Zeerust; I walked under the stars, overwhelmed by the age-old sorrow of first love.

The Brothers

It is a true saying that man may plan, but that God has the last word (Oom Schalk Lourens said).

And it was no different with Krisjan Lategan. He had one aim, and that was to make sure that his farm should remain the home of Lategans from one generation to the next until the end of the world. This would be in about two hundred years, according to the way in which a church elder, who was skilled in Biblical prophecy, had worked it out. It would be on a Sunday morning.

Krisjan Lategan wanted his whole family and all his descendants around him, so that on the Last Day they could all stand up together in an orderly fashion. There was to be no unseemly rushing around to look for Lategans who had wandered off into distant parts. Especially with the Last Day being a Sunday and all. Krisjan Lategan was particular that a solemn occasion should not be marred by the bad language that always went with rounding up stray oxen on a morning when you had to trek.

Afterwards, when they brought the telegraph up to Nietverdiend, and they showed the church elder how they could tap out messages from as far away as Cape Town, the elder shook his head and said that he did not give the world a full two hundred years any more. And when in Zeerust he heard a talking machine that could sing songs and speak words just through your turning a handle, the elder said that the end of the world was now quite near.

And he said it almost as though he was glad.

It was then that Krisjan Lategan set about the construction of the family vault at the end of his farm. It was the kind of vault that you see on some farms in the Cape. There was a low wall around it, like the kind you build for a sheep fold, and the vault was only a few feet below the level of the ground, and you walked down steps to a wooden door fastened with a chain. Inside were tamboetie wood trestles for the coffins to go on. The trestles were painted with tar, to keep away the white ants.

It was a fine vault. Farmers came from many miles away to admire it. And, as always happens in such cases, after their first feelings of awe had worn off, the visitors would make remarks which, in the parts of the Marico near the Bechuanaland border, regularly aroused guffaws.

They said, yes, it was quite a nice house, but where was the chimney? They also said that if you got up in the middle of the night and reached your hand under the bed – well, the vault wasn't a properly fixed up kind of vault at all.

The remark Hans van Tonder made was also regarded as very clever. Pointing to the tar on the trestles, he said he couldn't understand why old Krisjan should be so concerned about keeping the white ants out.

"When you lie in your coffin, it's not by *ants* that you get eaten up," Hans van Tonder said. "You get ants in your shirt, maybe, but not in your shroud."

Krisjan Lategan's neighbours had a lot of things of this nature to say about his vault when it was newly-constructed. All the same, not one of them would have been anxious to go to the vault alone at night after Krisjan Lategan had been laid to rest in it.

And yet all Krisjan Lategan's plans came to nothing. Shortly after his death certain events occurred on his farm, as a result of which one of his two sons came to an untimely end, and his corpse was placed in the vault in a coffin that was much too long. And the other son fled so far out of the Marico that it would certainly not be possible to find him again before the Last Day. And even then, on the Day of Judgment, he would not be likely to push himself forward to any extent.

Everybody in the bushveld knew of the bitterness that there was between old Krisjan Lategan's two sons, Doors and Lodewyk, who were in all things so unlike each other. At their father's death the two brothers were in their twenties. Neither was married. Doors was a few years older than Lodewyk.

Lodewyk, the younger brother, was tall and good-looking, and his nature was adventurous. The elder brother, Doors, was a hunchback. He had short legs and unnaturally broad shoulders. He was credited with great strength. Because of his grotesque shape, the kafirs told stories about him that had to do with witchcraft, and that could not be true.

At his father's funeral, Doors, with his short stature and the shapeless hump on his back, looked particularly ungainly among the other pall-bearers, all straight and upstanding men of the veld. During the simple service before the open doors of the vault a child burst out crying. It was something of a scandal that the child wept out of terror of Doors Lategan's hunched figure, and not because of sorrow for the departed. When the child got home his parents gave him something else to cry about.

Soon afterwards Lodewyk Lategan left the farm for the diamond diggings at Doornpan. Before that the brothers had quarrelled violently in the mealie-lands. The kafirs said that quarrel had been about what cattle Lodewyk could take with him to the diggings. When Lodewyk went it was with the new wagon and the best span of oxen. And Doors said that if he ever returned to the farm he would kill him.

In that spirit the brothers parted. Tant Alie, old Krisjan Lategan's widow, remained on the farm with her elder son, Doors. She was an aging woman with no force of character. She came of a Cape family of which quite a few members were known to be "simpel", although nobody, of course, thought any the less of them on that account. They belonged to a sheep district, Tant Alie's family, and we of the Marico, who were cattle farmers, said that for a sheep farmer it was even a help if he was a bit soft in the head.

But whatever Tant Alie might have thought and felt about the estrangement that was between her sons, she did not ever discuss the matter.

Lodewyk left for the diamond fields in the company of Flippie Geel, who had a piece of government land at Koedoesrand that he was supposed to improve. About all he had done in that direction, so far, was to sell the galvanised iron watertank that he had found on the place. Flippie Geel was a good deal older than Lodewyk Lategan. For that reason it seems all the more surprising that he should have helped Lodewyk in his subsequent foolish actions. Perhaps Flippie Geel found that going with Lodewyk was easier than work.

From what came out afterwards, it would appear that Lodewyk

Lategan and Flippie Geel did not dig much on their claim. But they put in a lot of time in the bar, drinking wine that Lodewyk paid for through selling his trek oxen, a pair at a time.

Lodewyk Lategan was not the first Marico farmer who had gone to the diggings and had there been able to see the wonder of his red Afrikaner cattle being turned into red wine in front of his eyes and not by means of looking-glasses, either, such as they say that the conjuror uses for his tricks in the Zeerust hall at Nagmaal.

And when he was in his cups Lodewyk would think out many schemes for getting even with his brother, Doors, who, he said, had defrauded him of his share of the inheritance.

One day Lodewyk got hold of a plan that he decided to carry out. From this you can get some idea of how crack-brained the plans must have been that he didn't act on. Anyway, he got Flippie Geel to write to Doors that his brother Lodewyk had been killed in an accident on the diggings, and that his body was being sent home in a coffin by transport wagon. And a few days later a coffin, which Lodewyk had made to his size, arrived at the Lategan farm.

Inside the coffin, instead of a corpse, was a mealie-sack that Lodewyk and Flippie Geel had filled with gravel.

I can picture Lodewyk and Flippie getting blisters on their hands from filling the sack – since that was perhaps the only time, on the diggings, that the two of them had got down to working with a shovel.

It is difficult to know what plan Lodewyk Lategan had with the coffin. Of course, he was drunk nearly always during that period. And if, as he claimed, he had not inherited his due portion of the family property, it is nevertheless likely that he inherited a full share of his mother's weakness of mind. But he must surely have expected Doors to unscrew the lid of the coffin, if for no other reason than to make certain that his brother really was dead.

Lodewyk could surely not have foreseen Doors acting the way he did when the coffin was delivered on the front stoep of the Lategan homestead. Without getting up from the riempies chair on which he was sitting – well forward because of his hump – Doors shouted for the farm kafirs to come and fetch away the coffin.

"Take this box to the vault and put it on a trestle," Doors said. "And don't put the lock back."

He silenced his mother when she asked to be allowed to gaze for the last time on the face of her dead son.

The transport driver, who had helped to carry the coffin on to the stoep, and had stood bare-headed beside it in reverence for the dead, felt there was something out of place in the figure he cut. He pushed his hat firmly on to his head. Then he walked back to his team, a very amazed man.

There are some who say that Doors Lategan had second sight. Or if it wasn't second sight it was a depth of cunning that was as good as second sight. And he had guessed that his brother Lodewyk's body was not in the coffin.

At the time, however, the farmers of the neighbourhood naturally had no suspicions of this nature. And they said it was not right that Doors should be so unfeeling. They said that the least Doors could have done was to put a black mourning band round his arm when he went to the poort to pump water for his cattle. They said he could also, when he went to load the pigs into the crates for the market, have worn a piece of crepe trimming in his hat. There was no harm in showing respect, people said.

A few weeks later it was known that Lodewyk's ghost was haunting the Lategan farm. Several kafirs swore to having seen the ghost of Baas Lodewyk on moonlight nights. They had seen Baas Lodewyk's ghost by the vault. Baas Lodewyk's ghost was sitting on the low wall, they said. And if they hadn't known that it couldn't be, they would even have thought that what Baas Lodewyk's ghost was holding in its hand was a black bottle. There was another kafir who said that he had heard Baas Lodewyk's ghost singing. He didn't stay long enough to make sure what song it was, the kafir added.

But what were even better established were the times when Lodewyk's ghost was seen driving along the high road in the back of Flippie Geel's mule-cart that had a half-hood over the back seat. For even white people had seen Lodewyk's ghost riding in the back seat of Flippie Geel's mule-cart. It was known that Flippie Geel had recently returned to the Marico to improve his government land some more. He was now trying to sell a mealie-planter with green handles that he had also found on the place.

155

Because in life Lodewyk Lategan had been Flippie Geel's bosom friend, it was not considered surprising that Lodewyk's ghost should have been seen haunting the back seat of Flippie Geel's mule-cart. But they were glad for Flippie's sake that Flippie hadn't turned round. Lodewyk's ghost looked too awful, the people said who saw it. It was almost as though it was trying to hide itself away against the half-hood of the cart.

It was when Hans van Tonder, fighting down his fears, crept up to Flippie Geel's window, one night, that the truth came out. Hans van Tonder was prepared for almost any dreadful sight when he looked through the window of the rondavel. But what met his gaze was something more unholy than he could ever have imagined. He saw Lodewyk sitting with his feet on the table and a look of contentment on his face, eating ostrich biltong. Next day everybody in the Marico knew that Lodewyk Lategan was not dead – not unless the ostrich biltong had killed him in between, that was.

Shortly afterwards came the night when Doors's kafirs reported to him that they had seen Baas Lodewyk climbing through the barbed wire with a gun in his hands. Doors took down his Mauser from the wall and went into the veld.

Next morning, in the Lategan family vault, a sack of gravel had been replaced by a body, and the coffin-lid had been screwed on again. During the night one brother had been murdered. The other had fled. He was never caught.

Several days passed before the veld-kornet came to the Lategan farm. And then Tant Alie would not give him permission to open the coffin. And she was unexpectedly firm about it.

"One of my sons is in the vault and the other is a fugitive over the face of the earth," Tant Alie said. "I don't want to know which is which."

Nevertheless, Tant Alie had to give way when the veld-kornet came back with an official paper. To reach the coffin the veld-kornet had to pass by the sack of gravel, which had burst open at the top. He kicked the gravel about a few times on the not very hopeful off-chance of turning up a diamond. Then he unscrewed the lid. In the coffin that was much too long for him – although it was cramped for breadth – lay Doors, the hunchback brother, with a bullet in his heart.

But even before the veld-kornet opened the coffin it was known in the Marico that it was Doors, the elder brother that had been murdered. For when the younger brother, Lodewyk Lategan, fled from the district he drove off in Flippie Geel's mule-cart. Several people had seen Lodewyk driving along the highway in the night. And those people said that for Lodewyk's own sake they were glad that Lodewyk did not look round.

It was well for Lodewyk Lategan, they said, that he should drive off and not know that there was a passenger in the back seat. The passenger had broad shoulders and the starlight shone through his ungainly hump.

The Kafir Drum

Old Mosigo was the last of the drum-men left at Gaberones when they brought the telegraph wires on long poles to this part of the country (Oom Schalk Lourens said). You can hear some kafir drums going now, down there in the vlakte – there they are again . . . tom-tom-tom-*tom*-tom. There must be a big beer drink on at those huts in the vlakte. Of course, that's all the kafirs use their drums for these days – to summon the neighbours to a party. On a quiet night you can hear those drums from a long distance away. From as far as the Bechuanaland border sometimes.

But there was a time when the voice of the kafir drum travelled right across Africa. I can still remember how, many years ago, the kafirs received messages from thousands of miles away with their drums. The tom-tom men in every village understood the messages sent out by the drums of the neighbouring villages. Then in their turn they spread the message further, with the result that, if the news was important, the whole of Africa knew it within a few days. The peculiar thing about this was that even when such a message originated from a tribe with a completely strange language, the drum-man of the tribe receiving the message could still interpret it. In the old days there were two drum-men in each village. They were instructed in the code of the drum from boyhood, and then in their turn they taught the art of sending and receiving messages by drum to those who came after them.

No white man has ever been able to learn the language of the kafirs' drums. The only white man who ever had any idea at all of what the drums said – and even his knowledge about it was of the slightest – was Gerhardus van Tonder who regularly travelled deep into Africa with his brother, Rooi Willem.

Gerhardus van Tonder told me that he had asked the drum-men of several tribes to teach him the meaning of the sounds they beat out on their tom-toms.

158

"But you know yourself how ignorant a kafir is," Gerhardus van Tonder said to me. "I could never understand what the drummen tried over and over again to explain to me. Even when a drum-man told me the same thing up to ten times I still couldn't grasp it. So thick-skulled are they."

Nevertheless Gerhardus said that, because he heard the same message so often, he was able, later on, to make it out whenever the drums broadcast the message that his brother, Rooi Willem, had shot an elephant dead. But one day an elephant trampled Rooi Willem to death. Gerhardus listened to the message that the drums sent out after that. It was exactly the same as all those earlier messages, Gerhardus said. Only, it was the other way around.

Even in those days the prestige of the drum-man had fallen considerably, because a mission station had been started at Gaberones, and the missionaries had brought with them their own message which came into conflict with the heathen news from Central Africa. But when the telegraph wires were brought up here from Cape Town, taken past the Groot Marico and into the Protectorate – then everyone knew that, so to speak, the days of the kafir drum-man were numbered.

Yet on one occasion when I spoke to old Mosigo about the telegraph, what he had to say was: "The drum is better than the copper wire that you white men bring on poles across the veld. I don't need copper wire for my drum's messages. Or long poles with rows of little white medicine bottles on them either."

But whatever Mosigo thought, the authorities had had the copper wires brought as far as Nietverdiend. A little post office had then been built on Jurie Bekker's farm, and a young telegraph operator from Pretoria appointed to serve as postmaster. This young man had arranged for a colleague in Pretoria to telegraph to him, from time to time, items from the newspapers. By means of these telegrams, which were pinned up on a notice board in the post office, we who live in this part of the bushveld kept in touch with the outside world.

The telegrams were all very short. In one of them we read of President Kruger's visit to Johannesburg and what he said, at a public meeting, about the Uitlanders.

"If that is all that the President could say about the Uitlanders," said Hans Grobler, "namely, 'that they are a pest stop and that they should be more heavily taxed stop and that a miners' procession threw bottles stop,' then I think that at the next elections I will simply vote for General Joubert. And why do these telegrams always repeat the word 'stop' so monotonously?"

Those of us who were in the post office at the time agreed with Hans Grobler. Moreover we said that not only did we need a better president, but a better telegraph operator as well. We also agreed that extending the telegraph service to Nietverdiend was a waste of hundreds of miles of copper wire, not to speak, even, of all those long poles.

When we mentioned this to the telegraph operator, he looked from one to the other of us, thoughtfully, for a few moments, and then he said, "Yes. Yes, I think it has been a waste."

Thereupon At Buitendag made a remark that we all felt was very sensible. "I can't read or write," he declared, "and I don't know what it is, exactly, that you are talking about. But I know that the best sort of news that I and my family used to get in the old days was the messages the kafirs used to thump out on their drums. I am not ashamed to say that I and my wife brought up seven sons and three daughters on nothing but that kind of news. I still remember the day old Mosigo – even in those days he was old already – received the message about the three tax collectors who got eaten by crocodiles when their boat was upset on the Zambesi . . ."

"And that sort of news was worth getting," Hans Grobler interrupted him. "I don't mean that we would be *pleased* if three tax collectors got eaten by crocodiles" – and we all said "Oh, no," and guffawed – "They are also human. The tax collectors, I mean. But my point is that that sort of news was *news*. That is something that we understand. But look at this telegram. About 'the fanatic who fired at the King of Spain stop and missed him by less than two feet stop'. What use is a message like that to us bushveld Boers? And what sort of a thing is a fanatic, anyway?"

As a result of the conversations at the post office I decided to look up Mosigo, the last of the drum-men at Gaberones.

I found him sitting in front of his hut. The wrinkles on his face were countless. They made me think of the kafir footpaths that go twisting across the length and breadth of Africa, and that you can follow for mile after mile and day after day, and that never come to an end. And I thought how the messages that Mosigo received through his drum came from somewhere along the farthest paths that the kafirs followed across Africa, getting footsore on the way.

He was busy thumping his old drum. Tom-tom tom-tom, it went. It sounded almost like a voice to me. Now and again it seemed as if there floated on the wind a sound from very far away, which was either an answer to Mosigo's message, or the echo of his drum. But it wasn't like in the old days, when you could hear clearly how the message of one drum was taken up and spread over koppies and vlaktes by other drums. Anyone could see that there were not so many drum-men left in the bushveld, these days. And the reducing of their numbers wasn't because the chiefs had had them thrown to the vultures for bringing bad news.

It could only be due to the competition of the white man's telegraph wires.

I carried on a long conversation with old Mosigo, and in the course of it I told him about the King of Spain. And Mosigo said to me that he did not think much of that kind of news, and if that was the best the white man could do with his telegraph wires, then the white man still had a lot to learn. The telegraph people could come right down to his hut and learn. Even though he did not have a yellow rod – like they had shown him on the roof of the post office – to keep the lightning away, but only a piece of python skin, he said.

And looking at Mosiga's wrinkles I considered that he must have more understanding of things than that young upstart of a telegraph operator who had only been out of school for three or four years at the most. And who always put the word "stop" in the middle of a message – a clear sign of his general uncertainty.

Even so, although I did not myself have a high opinion of the telegraph, I was not altogether pleased that an old kafir like Mosigo should speak lightly of an invention that came out of the white man's brain. And so I said that the telegraph was still quite a new thing and that it would no doubt improve in time. Perhaps how it would improve quite a lot would be if they sacked that young telegraph operator at Nietverdiend for a start, I said.

That young telegraph operator was too impertinent, I said.

Mosigo agreed that it would help. It was a very important

thing, he said, that for such work you should have the right sort of person. It was no good, he explained, having news told to you by a man who was not suited to that kind of work.

"Another thing that is important is having the right person to tell the news to," Mosigo went on. "And you must also consider well concerning whom the news is about. Take that King, now, of whom you have told me, that you heard of at Nietverdiend through the telegraph. He is a great chief, that King, is he not?"

I said to Mosigo that I should imagine he must be a great chief, the King of Spain. I couldn't know for sure, of course, you can't really, with foreigners.

"Has he many herds of cattle and many wives hoeing in the bean-fields?" Mosigo asked. "Do you know him well, this great chief?"

I told Mosigo that I did not know the King of Spain to speak to, since I had never met him. But if I did meet him – I was going on to explain, when Mosigo said that was exactly what he meant. "What is the good of hearing about a man," he asked, "unless you know who that man *is*? When the telegraph operator told you about that big chief, he told it to the wrong man."

And he fell to beating his drum again.

From then on I went regularly to visit Mosigo in order to find out what was happening in the world. We still read on the notice board in the post office about what had happened in, for instance, Russia – where a fanatic had opened fire on the Emperor "and missed him by one foot stop." We began to infer from the telegrams that a fanatic was someone who couldn't aim very well. But to get news that really meant something I had always, afterwards, to go and visit Mosigo.

Thus it happened that one afternoon, when I visited Mosigo on my way back from the post office, and found him again sitting in front of his hut before his drum, he told me that there would be no more news coming over his drum, because of a message about the death of a drum-man that he had just received.

It was a message that had come from a great distance, he said.

Still the following week I again rode over to Gaberones. It was after I had read a telegram on the notice board in the post office that said that a fanatic had missed the French President "by more than twenty feet."

And when I again rode away from Gaberones, where, this time, I had not seen Mosigo but had seen instead his drum, on which the skin stretched across the wooden frame had been cut, in accordance with the ritual carried out at the death of a drum-man – I wondered to myself on my way home, from how far, really, had it come – farther than France or Spain – that last message that Mosigo received.

The Picture of Gysbert Jonker

This tobacco-bag, now (oom Schalk Lourens said, producing a four-ounce linen bag with the picture on it of a leaping blesbuck – the trade-mark of a well-known tobacco company) well, it is very unusual, the way this tobacco-bag picture fits into the life-story of Gysbert Jonker.

I had occasion to think of that only the other day, when at the Zeerust bioscope during the last Nagmaal they showed a film about an English lord who had his portrait painted. And it seemed that after that only the portrait changed, with the years, as the lord grew older and more sinful.

Some of the young people, when they got back from the bioscope, came and called on me, on the kerk-plein, and told me what a good film it was. A few of them hinted that I ought also to go to the bioscope, now and again – say, once in two years, or so – to get new ideas for my stories.

Koos Steyn's younger son, Frikkie, even went so far as to say, straight out, that I should go oftener than just once every two years. A good deal oftener. And that I shouldn't see the same film through more than once, either.

"Important things are happening in the world, Oom Schalk," young Frikkie said. "You know, culture and all that. That's why you should go to a film like the one we have just seen. A film with artists in it, and all."

"Yes, artists," another young fellow said. "Like an artist that got pointed out to me last time I was in Johannesburg. With his wide hat and his corduroy trousers, he looked just like a Marico farmer, except that his beard was too wild. We don't grow our beards so long in these parts, any more, since that new threshing-machine with the wide hopper came in. That machine is so quick."

"That is the trouble with your stories, Oom Schalk," Frikkie Steyn continued. "The Boers in them all grew their beards too long. And the uppers of their veldskoens have got an old-fashioned look. Why can't you bring into your next story a young man with a pair of brown shop boots on, and" – hitching his pants up and looking down – "yellow and pink striped socks with a – "

"And a waistcoat with long points coming over the top part of the trousers," another young man interrupted him. "And braces with clips that you can make longer or shorter, just as you like."

Anyway, after Theunis Malan had demonstrated to me the difference between a loose and an attached collar, and then couldn't find his stud, and after an ouderling had come past just when another young man was using bad language because he couldn't get his head out through his shirt again – through somebody else having thoughtfully tied the shirt-tails together while the young man was explaining about a new kind of underwear – well, there wasn't much about their new Nagmaal clothes that these young men wanted me to leave out of my next story. And the ouderling, without knowing what was going on, and without trying to find out, even, merely shook his head solemnly as he went past.

And, of course, Frikkie Steyn, just to make sure I had it right, told the bioscope story of the English lord all over again – all the time that I was filling my pipe from a quarter-pound bag of Magaliesberg tobacco; the sort with the picture of the high-bounding blesbuck on it.

So I thought, well, maybe Gysbert was not an English lord. But I could remember the time when his portrait, painted in the most beautiful colours, hung in his voorkamer. And I also thought of the way in which Gysbert's portrait was on display on every railway platform and in every Indian shop in the country. And almost until the very end the portrait remained unchanged. It was only Gysbert Jonker who, despite all his efforts, altered with the years. But when the portrait did eventually change, it was a much more incredible transformation than anything that could have happened to the portrait of that lord in the bioscope story.

It was while we were sitting in the Indian store at Ramoutsa drinking coffee and waiting for the afternoon to get cool enough for us to be able to drive back home by mule and donkey-cart, that we first noticed the resemblance.

Our conversation was, as usual, of an edifying character. We spoke about how sensible we were to go on sitting in the Indian store, hour after hour, like that, and drinking coffee, instead of driving out in the hot sun and running the risk of getting sunstroke. Later on when some clouds came up, we were even more glad that we had not ventured out in our open carts, because everybody knows that the worst kind of sunstroke is what you get when the sun shines on to the back of your head through the clouds.

Of course, there were other forms of conveyance, such as Cape carts, we said. But that sort of thing only undermined you. Naturally, we did not wish to be undermined. We spoke about how the younger generation was losing its self-reliance through – and we started naming some of the things we saw on the shelves around us. Gramophones, we said. And paraffin candles in packets, we said, instead of making our own. And tubes with white grease that you squeeze at the end to polish your plates and spoons with, one of us said. No, it was to brush your teeth with, somebody else interrupted him. And we said that, well, whatever it was for, it was undermining. And we said that our own generation was being sapped, also.

After we had asked the Indian behind the counter to stand to one side, so that we could see better how we were being undermined, Hans Bekker pointed to a shelf holding tins of coffee. "Formerly we burnt and ground our own coffee," Hans Bekker said. "To-day – "

"Before I could walk," Andries Claassens said, "I used to shred my own tobacco from a black roll. I could cut up plug tobacco for my pipe before I could sharpen a slate-pencil. But now I have to sit with this little bag –"

I don't know who made the following observation, but we laughed at it for a long time. We looked from Andries Claassens's tobacco bag to the shelf on which dozens of similar bags were displayed. On each was the picture of a farmer with a black beard and a red-and-yellow checked shirt; and in his right hand, which was raised level with his shoulders, he held, elegantly if somewhat stiffly, a pipe. Perhaps you remember that picture, which did not

166

appear only on the tobacco bags, but was reproduced, also, in the newspapers, and stood on oblong metal sheets, enamelled in bright colours, in front of every store.

When our attention had been drawn to it, we saw the resemblance very clearly. In respect of both his features and his expression, the farmer on the tobacco bag was almost the exact image of Gysbert Jonker. Gysbert's beard was not so neatly trimmed, and his eyebrows were straighter; also, his mouth considerably larger than the man's on the picture. But in every other way – taking into consideration the difference in their dress – the likeness was astonishing.

Gysbert Jonker was there, in the Indian store, with us, when we made the discovery. He seemed very much interested.

"You will now have to push your ears in under the sweatband of your hat, in the city fashion," Hans Bekker said to Gysbert. "You can't have them bent anymore."

"And you will now have to hold your pipe up in the air, near to your shoulder, when you walk behind the plough," Andries Claassens added, "in your riding-breeches and leggings."

We were more than a little surprised at Gysbert's answer.

"It is absurd to think that I could do farm-work in that rigout," he replied. "But on Sundays, and some evenings after work, I shall wear riding-pants and top-boots. And it's a queer thing, but I have always wanted a shirt with red-and-yellow checks. In any case, it's the least I can do, in view of the fact that this tobacco company has honoured the Marico by making use of the portrait of the district's most progressive cattle farmer in this way. I suppose the tobacco firm selected me for this purpose because of the improvements I made to my cement-dip last year."

Gysbert Jonker added that next year he intended erecting another barbed-wire camp on the other side of the dam, and that he would bring this to the notice of the tobacco company as well.

We suddenly found that we had nothing more to say. And we were so taken aback at the way Gysbert responded to the purely accidental circumstance of his resembling the man in the picture that we were quite unable to laugh about it, even.

And I am sure that I was not the only Marico farmer, driving back home later that afternoon over the dusty road through the camelthorns, who reflected earnestly on the nature (and dangers) of sunstroke.

After a while, however, we got used to the change that had taken place in Gysbert Jonker's soul.

Consequently, with the passage of time, there was less and less said about the gorgeously-coloured shirts that Gysbert Jonker wore on Sundays, when he strolled about the front part of his homestead in riding-breeches and gaiters, apparently carefree and at ease, except that he held his pipe high up near his shoulder, somewhat stiffly. In time, too, the ouderling ceased calling on Gysbert in order to dissuade him from going about dressed as a tobacco advertisement on Sundays – a practice that the ouderling regarded as a desecration of the Sabbath.

In spite of everything, we had to admit that Gysbert Jonker had succeeded to a remarkable degree in imitating his portrait – especially when he started shaving the sides of his eyebrows to make them look more curved, and when he had cultivated a smile that wrinkled up his left cheek, half-way to his ear. And he used to smile carefully, almost as though he was afraid that some of the enamel would chip off him.

Jonker on one occasion announced to a number of acquaintances at a meeting of the Dwarsberg debating society, "Look at this shirt I have got on, for instance. Just feel the quality of it, and then compare it with the shirt on your tobacco-bag. I had my photo taken last month in Zeerust, in these clothes. I sent the photograph to the head office of the tobacco company in Johannesburg – and would you believe it? The tobacco people sent me, by the following railway-lorry, one of those life-sized enamelled pictures of myself painted on a sheet of iron. You know, the kind that you see on stations and in front of shops. I nailed it to the wall of my voorkamer."

Gysbert kept up this foolishness for a number of years. And it was, of course, this particular characteristic of his that we admired. We could see from this that he was a real Afrikaner, as obstinate as the Transvaal turfsoil. Even when, with the years, it became difficult for him to compete successfully with his portrait that did not age, so that he had to resort to artificial aids to keep his hair and beard black – then we did not laugh about it. We even sympathised with him in his hopeless struggle against the onslaughts of time. And we noticed that, the older Gysbert Jonker got, the more youthful his shirt seemed.

In the end, Gysbert Jonker had to hands-up of course. But he gave in only after his portrait had changed. And it was so stupendous a change that it was beyond the capacity even of Gysbert to try to follow suit. One day suddenly – without any kind of warning from the tobacco firm – we noticed, when we were again in the Indian store at Ramoutsa, that the picture of the farmer in riding-pants had disappeared from the tobacco-bags. Just like that. The farmer was replaced with the picture of the leaping blesbuck that you see on this bag, here. Afterwards, the blesbuck took the place of the riding pants farmer on the enamelled iron sheets as well.

Meanwhile, however, when it dawned on us that the tobacco company was busy changing its advertisement, we made many carefully considered remarks about Gysbert Jonker. We said that he would now, in his old age, have to start practising the high jump, in order to be able to resemble his new portrait. We also said that he would now have to paint his belly white, like the blesbuck's. We also expressed the hope that a leopard wouldn't catch Gysbert Jonker when he walked about the veld on a Sunday morning, dressed up like his new portrait.

Nevertheless, I had the feeling that Gysbert Jonker did not altogether regret the fact that his portrait had been unrecognisably changed. For one thing, he was now relieved of the strain of having all the time to live up to the opinion that the tobacco company had formed of him.

And although he removed the enamelled portrait from the wall of his voorkamer, and used it to repair a hole in the pigsty, and although he wore his gaudily-coloured shirts every day, now, and while doing the roughest kind of work, just so as to get rid of them – yet there were times, when I looked at Gysbert Jonker, that my thoughts were carried right back to the past. Most often this would happen when he was smoking. To the end, he retained something of his enamelled way by holding his pipe, his hand raised almost level with his shoulder, elegantly, but just a shade stiffly.

Some years later, when Gysbert Jonker was engaged in wearing out the last of his red-and-yellow checked shirts, I came across him at the back of his pigsty. He was standing near the spot where he had replaced a damaged sheet of corrugated iron with his tobacco-advertisement portrait.

And it struck me that in some mysterious way, Gysbert Jonker had again caught up with his portrait. For they looked equally shabby and dilapidated, then, the portrait and Gysbert Jonker. They seemed to have become equally sullied – through the years and through sin. And so I turned away quickly from that rusted sheet of iron, with the picture on it of that farmer with his battered pipe, and his beard that was now greying and unkempt. And his shirt that looked as patched as Gysbert Jonker's own. And his eyes that had grown as wistful.

Seed-Time and Harvest

At the time of the big drought (Oom Schalk Lourens said) Jurie Steyn trekked with what was left of his cattle to the Schweizer-Reineke district. His wife, Martha, remained behind on the farm. After a while an ouderling from near Vleisfontein started visiting Jurie Steyn's farm to comfort Martha. And as time went on, everybody in the Marico began talking about the ouderling's visits, and they said that the ouderling must be neglecting his own affairs quite a lot, coming to Jurie Steyn's farm so often, especially since Vleisfontein was so far away. Other people again, said that Vleisfontein couldn't be far enough away for the ouderling: not when Jurie Steyn got back, they said.

The ouderling was a peculiar sort of man, too. When some neighbour called at Jurie Steyn's farm, and Martha was there alone with the ouderling, and the neighbour would drop a hint about the drought breaking some time, meaning that Jurie Steyn would then be coming back to the Marico from the Schweizer-Reineke district with his cattle, then the ouderling would look very solemn, and he would say that it must be the Lord's will that this drought had descended on the Marico, and that he himself had been as badly stricken by the hand of the Lord as anybody and that the windmill pumped hardly enough water even for his prize large whites, and that in spite of what people might think he would be as pleased as anybody else when the rains came again.

That was a long drought. It was a very bitter period. But a good while before the drought broke the ouderling's visits to Martha Steyn had ceased. And the grass was already turning green in the heavy rains that followed on the great drought when Jurie Steyn got back to his farm-house with his wagon and his red Afrikaner cattle. And by that time the ouderling's visits to Martha were hardly even a memory any more.

But a while later, when Martha Steyn had a child again, there was once more a lot of talk, especially among the women. But there was no way of telling how much Jurie Steyn knew or guessed about what was being said about himself and Martha and the ouderling, and about his youngest child, whom they had christened Kobus.

It only seemed that for a good while thereafter Jurie Steyn seemed to be like a man lost in thought. And it would appear that he had grown absent-minded in a way that we hadn't noticed about him before. And it would seem, also, that his absent-mindedness was of a sort that did not make him very reliable in his dealings with his neighbours. It was almost as though what had been happening between the ouderling and Martha Steyn – whatever had been happening – had served to undermine not Martha's moral character but Jurie Steyn's.

This change that had taken place in Jurie Steyn was brought home to me most forcibly some years later in connection with some fence-poles that he had gone to fetch for me from Ramoutsa station. There was a time when I had regarded Jurie Steyn as somebody strong and upright, like a withaak tree, but it seemed that his character had gradually grown flat and twisted along the ground, like the tendrils of a pumpkin that has been planted in the cool side of a manure-pile at the back of the house. And that is a queer thing, too, that I have noticed about pumpkins. They thrive better if you plant them at the back of the house than in front. Something like that seemed to be the case with Jurie Steyn, too, somehow.

Anyway, it was when the child Kobus was about nine years old, and when Jurie Steyn's mind seemed to have grown all curved like a green mamba asleep in the sun, that the incident of the fence-poles occurred.

But I must first tell you about the school-teacher that we had there then. This school-teacher started doing a lot of farming in his spare time. Then he began taking his pupils round to his farm some afternoons, and he showed them how to plant mealies as part of their school subjects. We all said that that was nonsense, because there was nothing that we couldn't teach the children ourselves, when it came to matters like growing mealies. But the teacher said no, the children had to learn the theory of what

172

Nature did to the seeds, and it was part of natural science studies, and he said our methods of farming were all out of date, anyway.

We didn't know whether our methods of farming were out of date, but we certainly thought that there were things about the teacher's methods of education that were altogether different from anything we had come across so far. Because the school hours got shorter and shorter as the months went by, and the children spent more and more time on the teacher's farm, on their hands and knees, learning how to put things into the ground to make them grow. And when the mealies were about a foot high the teacher made the whole school learn how to pull up the weeds that grew between the mealies. This lesson took about a week: the teacher had planted so large an area. The children would get home from school very tired and stained from their lessons on the red, clayey sort of soil that was on that part of the teacher's farm.

And near the end of the school-term, when the dams were drying up, the children were given an examination in pumping water out of the borehole for the teacher's cattle.

But afterwards, when the teacher showed the children how to make a door for his pig-sty out of the school blackboard, and how to wrap up his eggs for the Zeerust market in the pages torn from their exercise books, we began wondering whether the more old-fashioned kind of school-teacher was not perhaps better – the kind of school-master who only taught the children to read and write and do sums, and left the nature-science job of cooking the mangolds for the pigs' supper to the kafirs.

And then there came that afternoon when I went to see Jurie Steyn about some fence-poles that he had gone to fetch for me from Ramoutsa station, and I found that Jurie was too concerned about something that the teacher had said to be able to pay much attention to my questions. I have mentioned how the deterioration in his moral characer took the form of making him absent-minded, at times, in a funny sort of a way.

"You can have the next lot I fetch," Jurie said. "I have been so worried about what the school-teacher said that I have already planted all your fence-poles – look, along there – by mistake. I planted them without thinking. I was so concerned about the school-master's impudence that I had got the kafirs to dig the holes and plant in the poles before I realised what I was doing. But I'll pay you for them, some time – when I get my cheque from the creamery, maybe. And while we are about it, I may as well use up the roll of barbed wire that is also lying at Ramoutsa station, consigned to you. You won't need that barbed wire, now."

"No," I said, looking at my fence poles planted in a long line. "No, Jurie, I won't need that barbed wire now. And another thing, if you stand here, just to the left of this anthill, and you look along the tops of the poles, you will see that they are not planted in a straight line. You can see the line bends in two places."

But Jurie said, no, he was satisfied with the way he had planted in my fence-poles. The line was straight enough for him, he said. And I felt that this was quite true, and that anything would be straight enough for him – even if it was something as twisted as a raw oxhide thong that you *brei* with a stick and a heavy stone slung from a tree.

"What did the school-teacher say about you?" I asked Jurie eventually, doing my best not to let him see how eager I was to hear if what had been said about him was really low enough.

"He said I was dishonest," Jurie answered. "He said . . ."

"How does he know?" I interrupted him quickly. "He's so busy on his farm there, with the harvesting, I didn't think he would have time to hear what is going on among us farmers. Did he make any mention of my fence-poles at all?"

"He didn't mean it that way," Jurie answered, standing to the side of the anthill and gazing into the distance with one eye shut. "No, I think those poles are planted in all right. When the school-master told me I was dishonest he meant it in a different sense. But what he said was bad enough. He said that my youngest son, Kobus, was dishonest, and that he feared that in that respect Kobus took after me."

I thought this was very singular. Did not the school-teacher know the story of the ouderling's visits to Jurie Steyn's wife, Martha, in the time of the big drought? Had Jurie Steyn no suspicions, either, about the boy, Kobus, not being his own child? But I did not let on to Jurie Steyn, of course, what my real thoughts were.

"So he said Kobus is dishonest?" I continued, trying to make

174

my voice sound disarming. "Why, did Kobus go along to Ramoutsa station with you, for my poles?"

"No," Jurie Steyn answered. "The school-master won't allow Kobus to stay away from school for a day – not until the harvesting is over. But I am sending Kobus to Ramoutsa on Saturday, by donkey-cart. I am sending him for that roll of barbed wire. And, oh, by the way, Schalk, while Kobus is in Ramoutsa, is there anything you would like him to get for you?"

I thanked Jurie and said, no, there was nothing for me at Ramoutsa that had not already been fetched. Then I asked him another question.

"Did the school-master perhaps say that you and Kobus were a couple of aard-varks?" I asked. "I daresay he used pretty rough language. Snakes, too, he must have said. I mean to say . . ."

"You are quite right," Jurie interrupted me. "That fourth pole from the end must come out. It's not in line."

"The whole lot must come out," I said, "and planted on my farm. That's what I ordered those poles for."

"That fourth pole of yours, Oom Schalk," Jurie repeated, "must be taken out and planted further to the left – I planted it in crooked because I was so upset by the school-master. It was only when I got home that I realised the cheek of the whole thing. I have a good mind to report the school-master to the Education Department for writing private letters with school ink. I'd like to see him get out of that one."

If the Education Department did not take any action after the school-master had used the front part of the school building to store his sweet-potatoes in, I did not think they would worry much about this complaint of Jurie Steyn's. By way of explanation the school-teacher told the parents that why he had to store the sweet-potatoes in that part of the school building for a while was because the prices on the Johannesburg market were so low, it was sheer robbery.

He also complained that the Johannesburg produce agents had no sense of responsibility in regard to the interests of the farmers.

"If I had so little sense of responsibility about my duties as a school-teacher," he said, "the Education Department would have sacked me long ago."

When the school-master made this remark several of the parents looked at him with a good deal of amazement.

These were the things that were passing through my mind while Jurie Steyn was telling me about the way the school-teacher had insulted him. I was anxious to learn more about it. I tried another way of getting Jurie to talk. I wanted to find out how much the school-master knew, and how much Jurie himself suspected, of the facts of Kobus's paternity. I felt almost as inquisitive as a woman, then.

"I once heard the school-master using very strong expressions, Jurie," I said, "and that was when he spoke to a Pondo kafir whom he had caught stealing one of the back wheels of his ox-wagon. I have never been able to understand how that kafir got the wheel off so quickly, because he didn't have a jack, as far as I know, and they say that the wagon had not been outspanned for more than two hours. But that was only a Pondo kafir without much understanding of the white man's language of abuse. No doubt what the school-teacher said about you and your son Kobus was . . ."

"It's possible to get a back wheel off an ox-wagon even if you haven't got a jack, so long as the wagon isn't too heavily loaded," Jurie said, without giving me a chance to finish, "and as long as you have got two other men to help you. Still, it would be interesting to know how the Pondo did it. Was it dark at the time, do you know?"

I didn't tell him. But it was getting dark on Jurie Steyn's farm. The deep shadows of the evening lay heavy across the thorn-bushes, and the farthest of my fence-poles had grown blurred against the sky. It seemed a strange thought to me that my fence-poles were that night for the first time standing upright and in silence, like the trees, awaiting the arrival of the first stars.

Jurie Steyn and I started walking towards the farm-house, in front of which I had left my mule-cart. The boy Kobus came out to meet us, and I could see from the reddish clay on his knees that he had studied hard at school that day.

"You look tired, Kobus," Jurie Steyn said. His voice suddenly sounded very soft. And in the dusk I saw the way that Kobus's eyes lit up when he took Jurie Steyn's hand. A singular variety of ideas passed through my mind, then, and I found that I no longer bore Jurie Steyn that same measure of resentment on account of his thoughtless way of acting with my fence-poles. I somehow felt that there were more important things in life than the question of what happened to my roll of barbed wire at Ramoutsa. And more important things than what had happened about the ouderling from near Vleisfontein.

Funeral Earth

We had a difficult task, that time (Oom Schalk Lourens said), teaching Sijefu's tribe of Mtosas to become civilised. But they did not show any appreciation. Even after we had set fire to their huts in a long row round the slopes of Abjaterskop, so that you could see the smoke almost as far as Nietverdiend, the Mtosas remained just about as unenlightened as ever. They would retreat into the mountains, where it was almost impossible for our commando to follow them on horseback. They remained hidden in the thick bush.

"I can sense these kafirs all around us," Veld-kornet Andries Joubert said to our "seksie" of about a dozen burghers when we had come to a halt in a clearing amid the tall withaaks. "I have been in so many kafir wars that I can almost *smell* when there are kafirs lying in wait for us with assegais. And yet all day long you never see a single Mtosa that you can put a lead bullet through."

He also said that if this war went on much longer we would forget altogether how to handle a gun. And what would we do then, when we again had to fight England?

Young Fanie Louw, who liked saying funny things, threw back his head and pretended to be sniffing the air with discrimination. "I can smell a whole row of assegais with broad blades and short handles," Fanie Louw said. "The stabbing assegai has got more of a selons-rose sort of smell about it than a throwing spear. The selons-rose that you come across in grave-yards."

The veld-kornet did not think Fanie Louw's remark very funny, however. And he said we all knew that this was the first time Fanie Louw had ever been on commando. He also said that if a crowd of Mtosas were to leap out of the bush on to us suddenly, then you wouldn't be able to smell Fanie Louw for dust. The veld-kornet also said another thing that was even better.

Our group of burghers laughed heartily. Maybe Veld-kornet

Joubert could not think out a lot of nonsense to say just on the spur of the moment, in the way that Fanie Louw could, but give our veld-kornet a chance to reflect, first, and he would come out with the kind of remark that you just had to admire.

Indeed, from the very next thing Veld-kornet Joubert said, you could see how deep was his insight. And he did not have to think much, either, then.

"Let us get out of here as quick as hell, men," he said, speaking very distinctly. "Perhaps the kafirs are hiding out in the open turf lands, where there are no trees. And none of this long tamboekie grass, either."

When we emerged from that stretch of bush we were glad to discover that our veld-kornet had been right, like always.

For another group of Transvaal burghers had hit on the same strategy.

"We were in the middle of the bush," their leader, Combrinck, said to us, after we had exchanged greetings. "A very thick part of the bush, with withaaks standing up like skeletons. And we suddenly thought the Mtosas might have gone into hiding out here in the open."

You could see that Veld-kornet Joubert was pleased to think that he had, on his own, worked out the same tactics as Combrinck, who was known as a skilful kafir-fighter. All the same, it seemed as though this was going to be a long war.

It was then that, again speaking out of his turn, Fanie Louw said that all we needed now was for the commandant himself to arrive there in the middle of the turf lands with the main body of burghers. "Maybe we should even go back to Pretoria to see if the Mtosas aren't perhaps hiding in the Volksraad," he said. "Passing laws and things. You know how cheeky a Mtosa is."

"It can't be worse than some of the laws that the Volksraad is already passing now," Combrinck said, gruffly. From that we could see that why he had not himself been appointed commandant was because he had voted against the President in the last elections.

By that time the sun was sitting not more than about two Cape feet above a tall koppie on the horizon. Accordingly, we started looking about for a place to camp. It was muddy in the turf lands, and there was no fire-wood there, but we all said that we did not mind. We would not pamper ourselves by going to sleep in the thick bush, we told one another. It was war time, and we were on commando, and the mud of the turf lands was good enough for *us*, we said.

It was then that an unusual thing happened.

For we suddenly did see Mtosas. We saw them from a long way off. They came out of the bush and marched right out into the open. They made no attempt to hide. We saw in amazement that they were coming straight in our direction, advancing in single file. And we observed, even from that distance, that they were unarmed. Instead of assegais and shields they carried burdens on their heads. And almost in that same moment we realised, from the heavy look of those burdens, that the carriers must be women.

For that reason we took our guns in our hands and stood waiting. Since it was women, we were naturally prepared for the lowest form of treachery.

As the column drew nearer we saw that at the head of it was Ndambe, an old native whom we knew well. For years he had been Sijefu's chief counsellor. Ndambe held up his hand. The line of women halted. Ndambe spoke. He declared that we white men were kings among kings and elephants among elephants. He also said that we were ringhals snakes more poisonous and generally disgusting than any ringhals snake in the country.

We knew, of course, that Ndambe was only paying us compliments in his ignorant Mtosa fashion. And so we naturally felt highly gratified. I can still remember the way Jurie Bekker nudged me in the ribs and said, "Did you hear that?"

When Ndambe went on, however, to say that we were filthier than the spittle of a green tree toad, several burghers grew restive. They felt that there was perhaps such a thing as carrying these tribal courtesies a bit too far.

It was then that Veld-kornet Joubert, slipping his finger inside the trigger guard of his gun, requested Ndambe to come to the point. By the expression on our veld-kornet's face, you could see that he had had enough of compliments for one day.

They had come to offer peace, Ndambe told us then.

What the women carried on their heads were presents.

At a sign from Ndambe the column knelt in the mud of the turf land. They brought lion and zebra skins and elephant tusks, and beads and brass bangles and, on a long mat, the whole haunch of a red Afrikaner ox, hide and hoof and all. And several pigs cut in half. And clay pots filled to the brim with white beer. And also – and this we prized most – witchdoctor medicines that protected you against *goël* spirits at night and the evil eye.

Ndambe gave another signal. A woman with a clay pot on her head rose up from the kneeling column and advanced towards us. We saw then that what she had in the pot was black earth. It was wet and almost like turf soil. We couldn't understand what they wanted to bring us that for. As though we didn't have enough of it, right there where we were standing and sticking to our veldskoens, and all. And yet Ndambe acted as though that was the most precious part of the peace offerings that his chief, Sijefu, had sent us.

It was when Ndambe spoke again that we saw how ignorant he and his chief and the whole Mtosa tribe were, really.

He took a handful of soil out of the pot and pressed it together between his fingers. Then he told us how honoured the Mtosa tribe was because we were waging war against them. In the past they had only had flat-faced Mshangaans with spiked knobkerries to fight against, he said, but now it was different. Our veld-kornet took half a step forward, then, in case Ndambe was going to start flattering us again. So Ndambe said, simply, that the Mtosas would be glad if we came and made war against them later on, when the harvests had been gathered in. But in the meantime the tribe did not wish to continue fighting.

It was the time for sowing.

Ndambe let the soil run through his fingers, to show us how good it was. He also invited us to taste it. We declined.

We accepted his presents and peace was made. And I can still remember how Veld-kornet Joubert shook his head and said, "Can you beat the Mtosas for ignorance?"

And I can still remember what Jurie Bekker said, also. That was when something made him examine the haunch of beef more closely, and he found his own brand mark on it.

It was not long afterwards that the war came against England.

By the end of the second year of the war the Boer forces were in a very bad way. But we would not make peace. Veld-kornet Joubert was now promoted to commandant. Combrinck fell in the battle before Dalmanutha. Jurie Bekker was still with us. And so was Fanie Louw. And it was strange how attached we had grown to Fanie Louw during the years of hardship that we went through together in the field. But up to the end we had to admit that, while we had got used to his jokes, and we knew there was no harm in them, we would have preferred it that he should stop making them.

He did stop, and for ever, in a skirmish near a block-house. We buried him in the shade of a thorn-tree. We got ready to fill in his grave, after which the Commandant would say a few words and we would bare our heads and sing a psalm. As you know, it was customary at a funeral for each mourner to take up a handful of earth and fling it in the grave.

When Commandant Joubert stooped down and picked up his handful of earth, a strange thing happened. And I remembered that other war, against the Mtosas. And we knew – although we would not say it – what was now that longing in the heart of each of us. For Commandant Joubert did not straightaway drop the soil into Fanie Louw's grave. Instead he kneaded the damp ground between his fingers. It was as though he had forgotten that it was funeral earth. He seemed to be thinking not of death then, but of life.

We patterned after him, picking up handfuls of soil and pressing it together. We felt the deep loam in it, and saw how springy it was, and we let it trickle through our fingers. And we could remember only that it was the time for sowing.

I understood then how, in an earlier war, the Mtosas had felt, they who were also farmers.

Other Stories

The Missionary

That kafir carving hanging on the wall of my voorkamer? (Oom Schalk Lourens said.) It's been there many years. It was found in the loft of the pastorie at Ramoutsa after the death of the Dutch Reformed missionary there, Reverend Keet. Of course, he was a sick man before he came here. Therefore, there may be nothing unusual in the circumstances of his death. Anyway, I'll tell you all I know about it. You can then judge for yourself.

To look at, that wooden figure is just one of those things that a kafir woodcarver cuts out of soft wood, like mdubu or mesetla. But because I knew him quite well, I can still see a rough sort of resemblance to Reverend Keet in that carving, even though it is now discoloured with age and the white ants have eaten away parts of it. I first saw this figure in the study of the pastorie at Ramoutsa when I went to call on Reverend Keet. And when, after his death, the carving was found in the loft of the pastorie, I brought it here. I kept it in memory of a man who had strange ideas about what he was pleased to call Darkest Africa.

Reverend Keet had not been at Ramoutsa very long. Before that he had worked at a mission station in the Cape. But, as he told us, ever since he had paid a visit to the Marico district, some years before, he had wanted to come to the Northern Transvaal. He said he had obtained, in the bushveld along the Malopo River, a feeling that here was the real Africa.

On his previous visit here Reverend Keet had stayed long enough to meet Elsiba Grobler, the daughter of Thys Grobler of Drogedal. Afterwards he sent for Elsiba to come down to the Cape to be his bride.

And so we thought that the missionary had remembered with affection the scenes that were the setting for his courtship. And that that was why he came back here. So you can imagine how disappointed we were when Reverend Keet said there was a spirit of evil in these parts that he believed it was his mission to overcome. We who had lived in the Marico for the greater part of our lives wondered much as to what it was that was going on in his soul. Reverend Keet had a thin neck and a fat stomach and an unhealthy colour. So we thought that perhaps his illness was responsible for his state of mind.

Nevertheless, I found it interesting to listen to him, just because he had such peculiar ways. And so I called on him quite regularly when I passed the mission station on my way back from the Indian store at Ramoutsa.

Reverend Keet and I used to sit in his study, where the curtains were half-drawn, as they were in the whole pastorie. I supposed it was to keep out the bright sunshine that Darkest Africa is so full of. I told him that I thought he would feel better if he got out among the trees and the grass oftener.

"Yesterday a kafir child hurt his leg falling out of a withaak tree," Reverend Keet said. "And the parents didn't bring the child here so that Elsiba or I could bandage him up. Instead, they said there was a devil in the withaak. And so they got the witch-doctor to fasten a piece of crocodile skin to the child's leg, to drive away the devil."

So I said that that just showed you how ignorant a kafir was. They should have fastened the crocodile skin to the withaak, instead, like the old people used to do. "The devil isn't in the kafir child but in the withaak," I said. "Though, goodness knows, the average kafir child has got enough devils in his skin!" I added that a length of leopard-entrail tied to the trunk was best for driving a devil out of a maroela.

Reverend Keet did not answer. He just shook his head and looked at me in a pitying sort of a way, so that I felt sorry I had spoken.

To change the subject I pointed to a kafir wood-carving standing on a table in a corner of the study. That same wood-carving you see to-day hanging on the wall of my voorkamer.

"Here's now something that we want to encourage," Reverend Keet said. "Through the teaching of craft we can perhaps bring enlightenment to these parts. The kafirs here seem to have a natural talent for wood-carving. I have asked Willem Terreblanche to write to the education department for a text-book on the subject. It will be another craft that we can teach to the children at the school." Willem Terreblanche was the assistant teacher at the mission station. "Anyway, it will be more useful than the things to make that were explained in the last text-book we got," Reverend Keet went on, half to himself. Then it was as though an idea struck him. "Oh, by the way," he asked, "would you perhaps like, say, a few dozen paper serviettes with green tassels to take home with you? They are free."

I declined his offer in some haste.

Reverend Keet started talking about that carving again.

"You wouldn't think it was meant for me, now, would you?" he asked. And because I am always polite, that way, I said no, certainly not. "I mean, just look at the top of the body," he said. "It's like a sack of potatoes. Does the top part of *my* body look like a sack of potatoes?" And once again I said no, oh, no.

Reverend Keet laughed, then – rather loudly, I thought – at the idea of that wood-carver's ignorance. I laughed quite loudly, also, to make it clear that I, too, thought that that kafir wood-carver was very uneducated.

"All the same, for a raw kafir who has had no training," the missionary continued, "it's not bad. But take that self-satisfied sort of smile, now, that he put on my face. It only came out that way because the kafir who made the carving lacks the disciplined skill to carve my features as they really are."

I thought, well, maybe that Bechuana didn't have much of what Reverend Keet called disciplined skill. But I did think he had a pretty shrewd idea how to carve a wooden figure of Rev. Keet.

"If a kafir had the impudence to make a likeness like that of me, with such big ears and all," I said to Reverend Keet, "I would kick him in the ribs. I would kick him for being so ignorant, I mean." I went on to say that the figure was carved out of mesetla and that the kafirs used the wood of that tree in their magic rituals for making black spells with.

"Because they are so ignorant," I again added quickly. For I could see that Reverend Keet was going to shake his head once more, at the thought of a white man having fallen so low as to believe in heathen superstitions.

It was then that Elsiba brought us in our coffee. Although she was now the missionary's wife, I still thought of her as Elsiba, a bushveld girl whom I had seen grow up.

187

"You've still got that thing there," Elsiba said to her husband, after she had greeted me. "I won't have you making a fool of yourself. Every visitor to the pastorie who sees this carving goes away laughing at you."

"They laugh at the kafir who made it, Elsiba, because of his lack of disciplined skill," Reverend Keet said, drawing himself up in his chair.

"Anyway, I am taking it out of here," Elsiba answered.

I had since then often thought of that scene. Of the way Elsiba Keet walked from the room, with the carving standing upright on the tray she had carried the coffee-cups on. Because of its big feet the wooden figure did not fall over when Elsiba flounced out with the tray. And in its stiff, wooden bearing the figure seemed to be expressing the same sorrow at the kafir wood-carver's lack of training that Reverend Keet himself felt.

I remained in the study a long time. And all the while the missionary talked of the spirit of evil that hung over the Marico like a heavy blanket. It was something brooding and oppressive, he said, and it did something to the souls of men. He asked me whether I hadn't noticed it myself.

So I told him that I had. I said that he had taken the very words out of my mouth. And I proceeded to tell him about the time Jurie Bekker had impounded some of my mules that he claimed had strayed into his mealie lands.

"You should have seen Jurie Bekker the morning that he drove off my mules along the government road," I said. "An evil blanket hung over him, all right. You could almost see it. A striped kafir blanket."

I also told the missionary about the sinful way in which Niklaas Prinsloo had filled in those drought compensation forms for losses which he had never suffered, even. And about the time Gert Haasbroek sold me what he said was a pedigree Afrikaner bull, and that was just an animal he had smuggled through from the Protectorate, one night, with a whole herd of other beasts, and that died afterwards of grass-belly.

I said that the whole of the Marico district was just bristling with evil, and I could give him many more examples, if he would care to listen.

But Reverend Keet said that that was not what he meant. He

188

said he was talking of the unnatural influence that hovered over this part of the country. He had felt those things particularly at the swamps by the Malopo, he said, with the green bubbles coming up out of the mud and with those trees that were like shapes oppressing your mind when it is fevered. But it was like that everywhere in the bushveld, he said. With the sun pouring down at midday, for instance, and the whole veld very still, it was yet as though there was a high black wind, somewhere. And he felt a chill in all his bones, he said, and it was something unearthly.

It was interesting for me to hear Reverend Keet talk like that. I had heard the same sort of things before from strangers. I wanted to tell him what he could take for it. But because the remedy I knew of included part of a crocodile's tooth ground fine and soaked in vinegar I felt that Reverend Keet might form a still lower opinion of me.

"Even here in this study, where I am sitting talking to you," he added, "I can sense a baleful influence. It is some form of – of something skulking, somehow." I knew, of course, that Reverend Keet was not referring in an underhand way to my presence there in his study. He was too religious to do a thing like that. Nevertheless, I felt uncomfortable. Shortly afterwards I left.

On my way back in the mule-cart I passed the mission school. And I thought then that it was funny that Elsiba was so concerned that a kafir should not make a fool of her husband with a wood-carving of him. Because she did not seem to mind making a fool of him in another way. From the mule-cart I saw Elsiba and Willem Terreblanche in the doorway of the school-room. And from the way they were holding hands I concluded that they were not discussing the making of paper serviettes with green tassels.

Still, as it turned out, it never came to any scandal in the district. For Willem Terreblanche left some time later to take up a teaching post in the Free State. And after Reverend Keet's death Elsiba allowed a respectable interval to elapse before she went to the Free State to marry Willem Terreblanche.

Some distance beyond the mission school I came across the Ramoutsa witch-doctor that Reverend Keet had spoken about. The witch-doctor was busy digging up roots on the veld for medicine. I reined in the mules and the witch-doctor came up to me. He had on a pair of brown leggings and carried an umbrella. Around his neck he wore a few feet of light-green tree-snake that didn't look as though it had been dead very long. I could see that the witch-doctor was particular about how he dressed when he went out.

I spoke to him in Sechuana about Reverend Keet. I told him that Reverend Keet said the Marico was a bad place. I also told him that the missionary did not believe in the cure of fastening a piece of crocodile skin to the leg of a child who had fallen out of a withaak tree. And I said that he did not seem to think, either, that if you fastened crocodile skin to the withaak it would drive the devil out of it.

The witch-doctor stood thinking for some while. And when he spoke again it seemed to me that in his answer there was a measure of wisdom.

"The best thing," he said, "would be to fasten a piece of crocodile skin on to the baas missionary."

Then the witch-doctor told me of a question that the Reverend Keet had asked him, and that surprised me a great deal.

Nevertheless, I have often since then thought of how almost inspired Reverend Keet was when he said that there was evil going on around him, right here in the Marico. In his very home – he could have said. With the curtains half-drawn and all. Only, of course, I don't suppose he meant it that way.

Yet I have also wondered if, in the way that he did mean it – when he spoke of those darker things that he claimed were at work in Africa – I wonder if there, too, Reverend Keet was as wide off the mark as one might lightly suppose. And it seemed to me that the witch-doctor might have been speaking the truth when he told me that the missionary had asked him certain strange questions. That thought occurred to me after Reverend Keet's death and Elsiba's departure. In fact, it was when the new missionary took over the pastorie at Ramoutsa and this wood-carving was found in the loft. But as I have said, Reverend Keet was a sick man before he came here. So his death might have had nothing to do with all this.

Yet, before I hung up the carving where you see it now, I first took the trouble to pluck off the lock of Reverend Keet's hair that had been glued to it. And I also pulled out the nails that Elsiba must have driven into the head and heart.

A Bekkersdal Marathon

At Naudé, who had a wireless set, came into Jurie Steyn's voor-kamer, where we were sitting waiting for the railway lorry from Bekkersdal, and gave us the latest news. He said that the newest thing in Europe was that young people there were going in for non-stop dancing. It was called marathon dancing, At Naudé told us, and those young people were trying to break the record for who could remain on their feet longest, dancing.

We listened for a while to what At Naudé had to say, and then we suddenly remembered a marathon event that had taken place in the little dorp of Bekkersdal – almost in our midst, you could say. What was more, there were quite a number of us sitting in Jurie Steyn's post office, who had actually taken part in that non-stop affair, and without knowing that we were breaking re-cords, and without expecting any sort of a prize for it, either.

We discussed that affair at considerable length and from all angles, and we were still talking about it when the lorry came. And we agreed that it had been in several respects an unusual occurrence. We also agreed that it was questionable if we could have carried off things so successfully that day if it had not been for Billy Robertse.

You see, our organist at Bekkersdal was Billy Robertse. He had once been a sailor and had come to the bushveld some years be-fore, travelling on foot. His belongings, fastened in a red handker-chief, were slung over his shoulder on a stick. Billy Robertse was journeying in that fashion for the sake of his health. He suffered from an unfortunate complaint for which he had at regular inter-vals to drink something out of a black bottle that he always carried handy in his jacket pocket.

Billy Robertse would even keep that bottle beside him in the organist's gallery in case of a sudden attack. And if the hymn the predikant gave out had many verses, you could be sure that about

191

half-way through, Billy Robertse would bring the bottle up to his mouth, leaning sideways towards what was in it. And he would put several extra twirls into the second part of the hymn

When he first applied for the position of organist in the Bekkersdal church, Billy Robertse told the meeting of deacons that he had learnt to play the organ in a cathedral in Northern Europe. Several deacons felt, then, that they could not favour his application. They said that the cathedral sounded too Papist, the way Billy Robertse described it, with a dome 300 ft. high and with marble apostles. But it was lucky for Billy Robertse that he was able to mention, at the following combined meeting of elders and deacons, that he had also played the piano in a South American dance hall, of which the manager was a Presbyterian. He asked the meeting to overlook his unfortunate past, saying that he had had a hard life, and anybody could make mistakes. In any case, he had never cared much for the Romish atmosphere of the cathedral, he said, and had been happier in the dance hall.

In the end, Billy Robertse got the appointment. But in his sermons for several Sundays after that the predikant, Dominee Wildhagen, spoke very strongly against the evils of dance halls. He described those places of awful sin in such burning words that at least one young man went to see Billy Robertse, privately, with a view to taking lessons in playing the piano.

But Billy Robertse was a good musician. And he took a deep interest in his work. And he said that when he sat down on the organist's stool behind the pulpit, and his fingers were flying over the keyboards, and he was pulling out the stops, and his feet were pressing down the notes that sent the deep bass tones through the pipes – then he felt that he could play all day, he said.

I don't suppose he guessed that he would one day be put to the test, however.

It all happened through Dominee Wildhagen one Sunday morning going into a trance in the pulpit. And we did not realise that he was in a trance. It was an illness that overtook him in a strange and sudden fashion.

At each service the predikant, after reading a passage from the Bible, would lean forward with his hand on the pulpit rail and give out the number of the hymn we had to sing. For years his manner of conducting the service had been exactly the same. He would say, for instance: "We will now sing Psalm 82, verses 1 to 4." Then he would allow his head to sink forward on to his chest and he would remain rigid, as though in prayer, until the last notes of the hymn died away in the church.

Now, on that particular morning, just after he had announced the number of the psalm, without mentioning what verses, Dominee Wildhagen again took a firm grip on the pulpit rail and allowed his head to sink forward on to his breast. We did not realise that he had fallen into a trance of a peculiar character that kept his body standing upright while his mind was a blank. We learnt that only later.

In the meantime, while the organ was playing over the opening bars, we began to realise that Dominee Wildhagen had not indicated how many verses we had to sing. But he would discover his mistake, we thought, after we had been singing for a few minutes.

All the same, one or two of the younger members of the congregation did titter, slightly, when they took up their hymn books. For Dominee Wildhagen had given out Psalm 119. And everybody knows that Psalm 119 has 176 verses.

This was a church service that will never be forgotten in Bekkersdal.

We sang the first verse and then the second and then the third. When we got to about the sixth verse and the minister still gave no sign that it would be the last, we assumed that he wished us to sing the first eight verses. For, if you open your hymn book, you'll see that Psalm 119 is divided into sets of eight verses, each ending with the word "*Pouse.*"

We ended the last notes of verse eight with more than an ordinary number of turns and twirls, confident that at any moment Dominee Wildhagen would raise his head and let us know that we could sing "Amen."

It was when the organ started up very slowly and solemnly with the music for verse nine that a real feeling of disquiet overcame the congregation. But, of course, we gave no sign of what went on in our minds. We held Dominee Wildhagen in too much veneration.

Nevertheless, I would rather not say too much about our feelings, when verse followed verse and *Pouse* succeeded *Pouse*, and still Dominee Wildhagen made no sign that we had sung long enough, or that there was anything unusual in what he was de-manding of us.

After they had recovered from their first surprise, the members of the church council conducted themselves in a most exemplary manner. Elders and deacons tiptoed up and down the aisles, whispering words of reassurance to such members of the congregation, men as well as women, who gave signs of wanting to panic.

At one stage it looked as though we were going to have trouble from the organist. That was when Billy Robertse, at the end of the 34th verse, held up his black bottle and signalled quietly to the elders to indicate that his medicine was finished. At the end of the 35th verse he made signals of a less quiet character, and again at the end of the 36th verse. That was when Elder Landsman tiptoed out of the church and went round to the *Konsistorie*, where the Nagmaal wine was kept. When Elder Landsman came back into the church he had a long black bottle half-hidden under his *manel*. He took the bottle up to the organist's gallery, still walking on tiptoe.

At verse 61 there was almost a breakdown. That was when a message came from the back of the organ, where Koster Claassen and the assistant verger, whose task it was to turn the handle that kept the organ supplied with wind, were in a state near to exhaustion. So it was Deacon Cronjé's turn to go tiptoeing out of the church. Deacon Cronjé was head warder at the local gaol. When he came back it was with three burly Native convicts in striped jerseys, who also went through the church on tiptoe. They arrived just in time to take over the handle from Koster Claassen and the assistant verger.

At verse 98 the organist again started making signals about his medicine. Once more Elder Landsman went round to the Konsistorie. This time he was accompanied by another elder and a deacon, and they stayed away somewhat longer than the time when Elder Landsman had gone on his own. On their return the deacon bumped into a small hymn book table at the back of the church. Perhaps it was because the deacon was a fat, red-faced man, and not used to tiptoeing.

At verse 124 the organist signalled again, and the same three members of the church council filed out to the Konsistorie, the deacon walking in front this time.

It was about then that the pastor of the Full Gospel Apostolic Faith Church, about whom Dominee Wildhagen had in the past used almost as strong language as about the Pope, came up to the front gate of the church to see what was afoot. He lived near our church and, having heard the same hymn tune being played over and over for about eight hours, he was a very amazed man. Then he saw the door of the Konsistorie open, and two elders and a deacon coming out, walking on tiptoe – they having apparently forgotten that they were not in church, then. When the pastor saw one of the elders hiding a black bottle under his manel, a look of understanding came over his features. The pastor walked off, shaking his head.

At verse 152 the organist signalled again. This time Elder Landsman and the other elder went out alone. The deacon stayed behind on the deacon's bench, apparently in deep thought. The organist signalled again, for the last time, at verse 169. So you can imagine how many visits the two elders made to the Konsistorie altogether.

The last verse came, and the last line of the last verse. This time it had to be "Amen." Nothing could stop it. I would rather not describe the state that the congregation was in. And by then the three Native convicts, red stripes and all, were, in the Bakhatla tongue, threatening mutiny. "Aa-m-e-e-n" came from what sounded like less than a score of voices, hoarse with singing.

The organ music ceased.

Maybe it was the sudden silence that at last brought Dominee Wildhagen out of his long trance. He raised his head and looked slowly about him. His gaze travelled over his congregation and then looking at the windows, he saw that it was night. We understood right away what was going on in Dominee Wildhagen's mind. He thought he had just come into the pulpit, and that this was the beginning of the evening service. We realised that, during all the time we had been singing, the predikant had been in a state of unconsciousness.

Once again Dominee Wildhagen took a firm grip of the pulpit rail. His head again started drooping forward on to his breast. But before he went into a trance for the second time, he gave out the hymn for the evening service. "We will," Dominee Wildhagen announced, "sing Psalm 119."

Birth Certificate

It was when At Naudé told us what he had read in the newspaper about a man who had thought all his life that he was White, and had then discovered that he was Coloured, that the story of Flippus Biljon was called to mind. I mean, we all knew the story of Flippus Biljon. But because it was still early afternoon we did not immediately make mention of Flippus. Instead, we discussed, at considerable length, other instances that were within our knowledge of people who had grown up as one sort of person and had discovered in later life that they were in actual fact quite a different sort of person.

Many of these stories that we recalled in Jurie Steyn's voorkamer as the shadows of the thorntrees lengthened were based only on hearsay. It was the kind of story that you had heard, as a child, at your grandmother's knee. But your grandmother would never admit, of course, that she had heard that story at *her* grandmother's knee. Oh, no. She could remember very clearly how it all happened, just like it was yesterday. And she could tell you the name of the farm. And the name of the landdrost who was summoned to take note of the extraordinary occurrence, when it had to do with a more unusual sort of changeling, that is. And she would recall the solemn manner in which the landdrost took off his hat when he said that there were many things that were beyond human understanding.

Similarly now, in the voorkamer, when we recalled stories of white children that had been carried off by a Bushman or a baboon or a werewolf, even, and had been brought up in the wilds and without any proper religious instruction, then we also did not think it necessary to explain where we had first heard those stories. We spoke as though we had been actually present at some stage of the affair – more usually at the last scene, where the child, now grown to manhood and needing trousers and a pair of braces and a hat, gets restored to his parents and the magistrate after studying the birth certificate says that there are things in this world that baffle the human mind.

And while the shadows under the thorn-trees grew longer the stories we told in Jurie Steyn's voorkamer grew, if not longer, then, at least, taller.

"But this isn't the point of what I have been trying to explain," At Naudé interrupted a story of Gysbert van Tonder's that was getting a bit confused in parts, through Gysbert van Tonder not being quite clear as to what a werewolf was. "When I read that bit in the newspaper I started wondering how must a man *feel*, after he has grown up with adopted parents and he discovers, quite late in life, through seeing his birth certificate for the first time, that he isn't White, after all. That is what I am trying to get at. Supposing Gysbert were to find out suddenly – "

At Naudé pulled himself up short. Maybe there were one or two things about a werewolf that Gysbert van Tonder wasn't too sure about, and he would allow himself to be corrected by Oupa Bekker on such points. But there were certain things he wouldn't stand for.

"All right," At Naudé said hastily, "I don't mean Gysbert van Tonder, specially. What I am trying to get at is, how would any one of us feel? How would any White man feel, if he has passed as White all his life, and he sees for the first time from his birth certificate that his grandfather was Coloured? I mean, how would he *feel*? Think of that awful moment when he looks in the palm of his hands and he sees . . ."

"He can have that awful moment," Gysbert van Tonder said. "I've looked at the palm of my hand. It's a White man's palm. And my finger-nails have also got proper half-moons."

At Naudé said he had never doubted that. No, there was no need for Gysbert van Tonder to come any closer and show him. He could see quite well enough just from where he was sitting. After Chris Welman had pulled Gysbert van Tonder back on to the *rusbank* by his jacket, counselling him not to do anything foolish, since At Naudé did not mean *him*, Oupa Bekker started talking about a White child in Schweizer Reineke that had been stolen out of its cradle by a family of baboons.

"I haven't seen that cradle myself," Oupa Bekker acknowledged, modestly. "But I met many people who have. After the child had been stolen, neighbours from as far as the Orange River came to look at that cradle. And when they looked at it they admired the particular way that Heilart Nortjé – that was the child's father – had gone about making his household furniture, with glued *klinkpenne* in the joints, and all. But the real interest about the cradle was that it was empty, proving that the child had been stolen by baboons. I remember how one neighbour, who was not on very good terms with Heilart Nortjé, went about the district saying that it could only have *been* baboons.

"But it was many years before Heilart Nortjé and his wife saw their child again. By *saw*, I mean getting near enough to be able to talk to him and ask him how he was getting on. For he was always too quick, from the way the baboons had brought him up. At intervals Heilart Nortjé and his wife would see the tribe of baboons sitting on a *rant,* and their son, young Heilart, would be in the company of the baboons. And once, through his field-glasses, Heilart had been able to observe his son for quite a few moments. His son was then engaged in picking up a stone and laying hold of a scorpion that was underneath it. The speed with which his son pulled off the scorpion's sting and proceeded to eat up the rest of the scorpion whole filled the father's heart of Heilart Nortjé with a deep sense of pride.

"I remember how Heilart talked about it. 'Real intelligence,' Heilart announced with his chest stuck out. 'A real baboon couldn't have done it quicker or better. I called my wife, but she was a bit too late. All she could see was him looking as pleased as anything and scratching himself. And my wife and I held hands and we smiled at each other and we asked each other 'Where does he get it all from?'

"But then there were times again when that tribe of baboons would leave the Schweizer Reineke area and go deep into the Kalahari, and Heilart Nortjé and his wife would know nothing about what was happening to their son, except through reports from farmers near whose homesteads the baboons had passed. Those farmers had a lot to say about what happened to some of their sheep, not to talk of their mealies and watermelons. And Heilart would be very bitter about those farmers. Begrudging his son a few prickly-pears, he said.

"And it wasn't as though he hadn't made every effort to get his son back, Heilart said, so that he could go to catechism classes, since he was almost of age to be confirmed. He had set all sorts of traps for his son, Heilart said, and he had also thought of shooting the baboons, so that it would be easier, after that, to get his son back. But there was always the danger, firing into a pack like that, of his shooting his own son."

"The neighbour that I have spoken of before," Oupa Bekker continued, "who was not very well disposed towards Heilart Nortjé, said that the real reason Heilart didn't shoot was because he didn't always know – actually *know* – which was his son and which was one of the more flat-headed kees-baboons."

It seemed that this was going to be a very long story. Several of us started getting restive ... So Johnny Coen asked Oupa Bekker, in a polite sort of a way, to tell us how it all ended.

"Well, Heilart Nortjé caught his son, afterwards," Oupa Bekker, said, "But I am not sure if Heilart was altogether pleased about it. His son was so hard to tame. And then the way he caught him. It was with the simplest sort of baboon trap of all ... Yes, *that* one. A calabash with a hole in it just big enough for you to put your hand in, empty, but that you can't get your hand out of again when you're clutching a fistful of mealies that was put at the bottom of the calabash. Heilart Nortjé never got over that, really. He felt it was a very shameful thing that had happened to him. The thought that his son, in whom he had taken so much pride, should have allowed himself to be caught in the simplest form of monkey-trap."

When Oupa Bekker paused, Jurie Steyn said that it was indeed a sad story, and it was no doubt, perfectly true. There was just a certain tone in Jurie Steyn's voice that made Oupa Bekker continue.

"True in every particular," Oupa Bekker declared, nodding his head a good number of times. "The landdrost came over to see about it, too. They sent for the landdrost so that he could make a report about it. I was there, that afternoon, in Heilart Nortjé's voorkamer, when the landdrost came. And there were a good number of other people, also. And Heilart Nortjé's son, half-tamed in some ways but still baboon-wild in others, was there also. The landdrost studied the birth certificate very carefully. Then the landdrost said that what he had just been present at surpassed ordinary human understanding. And the landdrost took off his hat in a very solemn fashion.

"We all felt very embarrassed when Heilart Nortjé's son grabbed the hat out of the landdrost's hand and started biting pieces out of the crown."

When Oupa Bekker said those words it seemed to us like the end of a story. Consequently, we were disappointed when At Naudé started making further mention of that piece of news he had read in the daily paper. So there was nothing else for it but that we had to talk about Flippus Biljon. For Flippus Biljon's case was just the opposite of the case of the man that At Naudé's newspaper wrote about.

Because he had been adopted by a Coloured family, Flippus Biljon had always regarded himself as a Coloured man. And then one day, quite by accident, Flippus Biljon saw his birth certificate. And from that birth certificate it was clear that Flippus Biljon was as White as you or I. You can imagine how Flippus Biljon must have felt about it. Especially after he had gone to see the magistrate at Bekkersdal, and the magistrate after studying the birth certificate, confirmed the fact that Flippus Biljon was a White man.

"Thank you *baas*," Flippus Biljon said. "Thank you very much *my basie*."

Day of Wrath

It was what At Naudé had read in the newspapers.

Somewhere in an overseas country the people in that part had come together in a barn to wait for the end of the world, which a holy woman had gone out of her way to prophesy for them would be quite soon.

"They stopped work and sold their land for – well, I don't quite remember, now how much they got for it, a morgen," At Naudé said. "But it went quite cheap. And so they just sat in the barn, waiting for the Day of Judgment."

Then Gysbert van Tonder said he wondered what those lands were like that the holy woman's followers had sold. Maybe it was just *brak* soil, and with ganna bushes. Well, that sort of ground you could keep, Gysbert van Tonder said. He had had experience of just that kind of lands. And what about turf soil, now, he asked – the sticky kind? There was a thing for you, too, he observed.

Thereupon Chris Welman said that if those people sitting in that overseas barn, there, wanted land so cheap that it was almost nothing a morgen – certainly not more than ten pounds a morgen, with two boreholes thrown in – then he himself was just the right man for them to come and talk to. Did the newspaper give the address of that barn, perhaps?

In the slight altercation that ensued between Gysbert van Tonder and Chris Welman (Gysbert van Tonder contending that he had thought of it first and that Chris Welman had no right to come and intrude, talking about ten pounds a morgen for a piece of koppie that you couldn't keep a goat alive on, not unless you fed the goat an old hat or a piece of shirt, every so often), At Naudé was able to explain, several times, that they had missed the whole point of what he was talking about. It wasn't the price of land that the newspaper story dealt with so much as the preparations that those people were making for the Day of Judgment.

"The End of the World," At Naudé stated majestically, *"Die laaste der dagen."*

He knew it would sound more solemn if he said it in Bible Nederlands instead of just in Afrikaans.

But by that time Chris Welman was saying to Gysbert van Tonder that Gysbert was pretty much like a goat himself, the way he had come butting in, and Gysbert van Tonder was saying that the way Chris Welman's trousers looked from the back, it would appear as though Gysbert had already been feeding parts of his trousers to the goats.

"Anyway, where's your shirt buttons?" Chris Welman asked of Gysbert van Tonder, sarcastically, "I suppose the ostriches ate them?"

We felt that this was an unfortunate quarrel, between Gysbert van Tonder and Chris Welman. We sensed that it was the kind of argument that wouldn't get either of them anywhere. Moreover, when it came to a matter of dress – or, rather, to a question of tabulating things that weren't there – why, we knew that we were none of us immune from thoughtless criticism.

The jagged missiles that Gysbert van Tonder and Chris Welman were hurling at each other on the score of the respective short-comings in their personal attire – well, a rusty old piece of that kind of weapon could wound any one of us, sitting in Jurie Steyn's voorkamer. And even if it wasn't aimed at you, and even if it got you only glancingly, it could make you feel bruised, all the same. More than one of us shifted uncomfortably on his *riempies* chair, then.

But it was when Chris Welman was talking about when Gysbert van Tonder had had a hair-cut last that Oupa Bekker took a firm hand in the proceedings.

We were more than a little surprised that, in spite of his deafness, Oupa Bekker should have followed the argument so well. We had noticed that about Oupa Bekker before, however – that he didn't really miss much about what was going on: not when he was personally affected.

"At Naudé has been talking about Judgment Day," Oupa Bekker said severely, at the same time moving his good velskoen forward, so as partly to hide the place in his other velskoen that was patched with a piece of rubber tubing. "And on the Day of Judgment we will none of us be judged by the *clothes* we're wearing at the time. We'll be judged by just what we are."

From the way Oupa Bekker said it, it sounded that that would be bad enough.

So Chris Welman said that he certainly hoped, for Gysbert van Tonder's own sake, that on the Last Day Gysbert would not be judged by the kind of clothes he was wearing. If Gysbert's clothes already looked like that now, Chris Welman said, he would rather not think how they would look on the Last Day. He just couldn't imagine anything more sinful, Chris Welman added. Not just offhand he couldn't, Chris Welman said.

Before Gysbert van Tonder could think of a suitable answer, Oupa Bekker went on to say that what really was sinful was the way Chris Welman had talked of wanting to sell his ground – asking ten pounds a morgen for it – to those people in a foreign country who didn't know any better.

"Religious people," Oupa Bekker said. "Sitting there in a barn because their prophetess woman had told them that it was the End of the World. And Protestant people, too, by the sound of it."

We agreed with Oupa Bekker that they were Protestants, by the sound of it.

"And just because Chris Welman wants to trek to Rhodesia, as we all know," Oupa Bekker announced, finally, "he doesn't ask even if they're Catholics, first, before he thinks of selling his farm to them, which we know isn't worth ten pounds a morgen, just because he wants to go to Rhodesia."

Chris Welman could only say that for those people to have his farm was better than their sitting in a barn, anyway. Whereupon Gysbert van Tonder said that he wasn't so sure.

Gysbert van Tonder also said that if Chris Welman got ten pounds a morgen for his farm, then it would be the end of the world.

Oupa Bekker agreed with Gysbert van Tonder. Oupa Bekker said that he knew Chris Welman's farm in the old days, when it was just concession ground. And he wouldn't be sure if he didn't even prefer that ground like it was in the old days, before Chris Welman had made what he called improvements on it, Oupa Bekker added.

It seemed queer that Oupa Bekker should be so very much against Chris Welman. But it was only when Oupa Bekker spoke again that we understood something of the reason for it. And we also realised in a deeper manner the truth of what we had in the course of time come to understand about Oupa Bekker's deafness: that Oupa Bekker was hardly at all deaf when there was talk going on in which he was personally affected.

"Take my own little place, now," Oupa Bekker said, "There it lies, on both sides of Pappegaai Poort. There's a bit of ground for you, now. For somebody that wants to make a new start, and that isn't afraid of a bit of hard work. Catholic or Protestant, there's now a –"

But Oupa Bekker didn't get any further. For by that time we were all laughing.

"Well, I only hope that on the Last Day I'm not found on your farm, Oupa Bekker," Chris Welman said. "Not when it comes to being judged, that is. And no matter what sort of clothes I had on, either. Even if I was wearing my black Nagmaal *manel*. I wouldn't fancy my chances much, if I was found walking on Judgment Day on any part of your farm. Not with all those khakibos and those erosion sloots, I wouldn't."

All the same, it was strange to think that Oupa Bekker, at his age, should also be toying with the idea of trekking to Rhodesia. Otherwise he would never want to sell his farm. It must be that Oupa Bekker had also heard about how much you could make out of tobacco, in Rhodesia. Perhaps he had also heard about how glad the Rhodesian government was to have Afrikaners trekking in there, so much so that they were asking questions about it in the Rhodesian Legislative Assembly almost every week.

It was only after At Naudé had spoken for some time again, trying to give us a clear picture of that prophetess woman and her followers waiting in the barn for the Last Day, that we began to understand properly what it meant.

And we started to think of Gabriel's Trumpet, then. And of the book in the tenth chapter of Revelations that St. John ate. And of the millions of people, the dead and the living, that would gather at the foot of Mount Zion. And the vials of wrath. And the fall of Babylon. And the beast with seven heads.

These were things you could not reflect on just lightly.

204

"I wonder why they were so quick to listen to their prophet woman, the people in that foreign part," Jurie Steyn commented at length, scratching his head at the same time. "I mean, there must have been a reason, why they heeded her words and sold up so quick. After all, there was nothing that she could prophesy to them that could be half as bad as what you can read for yourself in the last few pages of the Good Book. Things like the passing of the first world in pools of fire. I have read it more than once, for myself, in a time of drought."

Well, we were in entire agreement with Jurie Steyn, there. When there had been no rain in the Marico for three years, we said, and the last water in the borehole was drying up – if you could even call it water, with all that brack in it – well, it was comforting, we acknowledged, to sit on one's stoep and to read of the Day of Wrath and of the second seal being opened.

It made you feel quite happy then, we said, to think of all the awful things that were going to happen to the world: and to think that it was all just round the corner, too, from the way the holy St. John spoke.

We were suddenly able to understand something of what must have been going on in the minds of those foreign people, who listened to their prophetess woman. Seeing that we were farmers ourselves, we understood.

"I think I see what you're getting at, Jurie," At Naudé remarked, after a while. "You do get a bellyful of it, sometimes, don't you? After all, even if there isn't a drought, you do suddenly find, when you take a look over your farm, including the improvements you've made on it – "

"Especially the improvements," Chris Welman interjected bitterly, "no matter what Oupa Bekker says about them – "

"Anyway, you do get the feeling," At Naudé continued. "Revelations or no Revelations – that you've just got a bellyful."

Until that moment we had not understood properly, why it was that there was so much solace to be found in the last 20 chapters of the Good Book, ending up with "der volken daarin brengen."

If it was the End of the World, then, at least, the End of the World would be a change. And the lure of selling up and going to Rhodesia did not have much to do with tobacco-planting, but it was a thing as old as Africa.

205

"It's funny, now, about Policansky," Gysberg van Tonder remarked, "But last time I saw David Policansky, he told me he was looking for a buyer for his store. He wanted to trek out somewhere, right away from Bekkersdal he said. And you know what – from the way that David Policansky spoke, it sounded almost as though he has also been reading the New Testament, for drawing comfort. He wasn't talking much different from what we're talking now. He would sell out quite cheap, he said, too."